ISBN: 978-1519710048
ISBN-13: 1519710046

DEDICATION & ACKNOWLEDGEMENTS

This book is dedicated to the Goddesses who don't know they are goddesses. The Queens who don't know they are queens. And to the everyday girl next door who occasionally looks in the mirror and says, "I'm pretty damn awesome." Rock on sister. Rock on.

CONTENTS

"Keep knocking and the joy inside
will eventually open a window and
look out to see who's there."

~Rumi

INTRODUCTION
by Suki Eleuterio

I was lying in bed when the idea came to me. It was more of a whisper, a cool breeze brushing against my cheek and the words *"she loved herself."*

Through the window curtains I could see flecks of sunlight. It couldn't be more than seven o'clock because the sun was barely rising. I turned around and the whisper got louder, "she loved herself." Then more whispers, "book, you have to write a book, get other women involved, collaborate, share, create a dialogue, change lives." It was flooding my head all at once so I grabbed a pen to write it down.

This is what I call divine intervention. Divine messages. Channeling.

I knew instantly that this project was bigger than me. I knew it was being guided and presented through me so that other women could feel, and express, and release, and laugh and cry happy tears, or jump over obstacles. This book was part of a larger revolution to help women around the world recognize their souls. It doesn't get more important than that.

I could have stayed in bed and ignored the calls. I could have spent an extra hour catching up on my slumber but I knew I had to get up and act immediately.

How many times have you chosen to lay down even when you knew you should be standing up? How many times have you told yourself you're not good enough? Not smart enough? Not pretty enough?

We wrote this book to break the mold, change the internal dialogue, confront the feelings, and own our own strength. Step into that power.

And what did we find by writing this book? That self-love is hard; it takes time and commitment. That it is emotional, that it is raw, that it involves unpeeling the layers to get the true, authentic you. Our journeys are unique and yet so similar. It's comforting to know that even in your darkest hours there is another woman who has struggled through those same obstacles. We grow through our darkness. Our scars make us; they don't break us. And most of all, it's all right to be exactly who you are...flaws and all.

Each time we met – bonding together as goddesses, as sisters, as friends, and as co-creators, we felt a shift in the universe. We would hold hands and chant and meditate and bring only our highest of intentions into creating this book. A book made purely out of love.

We hope you will enjoy the book and these true, raw, honest stories that we have shared.

And above everything else, we hope this book makes you realize the love that you have been seeking is really already with you. It's been there all along.

Happy loving yourself,

Suki

LOVE MYSELF

A Letter to My Body

by Susan Araujo

My Dear Body,

We have been on quite the journey together.
I love and appreciate you more than ever
But...
Honestly, I have struggled to love you.

Everything around you made
You were really unhealthy at a young age.
You completely changed in a
Very short period of time.
I have a vivid memory of you.
I was looking at my arms...
The stretch marks, wondering how and when you got this
way.

I felt completely disconnected from you.
I felt so uncomfortable.
(I still do!)
I didn't appreciate you and honestly....
I despised you.

I couldn't stand looking at you.
Or to feel you.
Or to be you.
You were no longer healthy, athletic, and energetic.
It didn't feel right.

Ever since you became sick
I have felt uncomfortable.
I hated that feeling.
I don't like being fat.
It's an imbalance.
Lack of health.

I hate this feeling.

For the longest time
I was ashamed and afraid of exposing you.

I covered you.
As much as possible.
I wanted to hide you.
As much as possible.

I was embarrassed.

At some point in our journey,
I decided I no longer wanted to feel this way.
My feelings shifted to self-love.

With my newly acquired awareness and knowledge
I began to treat you with more respect.
You became healthier.
You changed!

You are no longer fat.

Your health improved.

However, you still hold remnants of the past.
Your scars are evident and your skin is no longer firm.

You still feel fat.

This is the harsh reality.
This is Yin.

But I welcome the Yang!

My feelings shifted to self-love.

My dear body,

I apologize for striking you down.

I thank you.
For growing in health.
For the opportunity to live a happier life.
For being the vehicle to my soul.

For helping me journey and experience
This magical and mysterious human experience.

Thank you for arms that experience loving, healing hugs.
Thank you for the smile you've given me to share joy with
loved ones.
Thank you for beautiful eyes that have the ability to gaze
into other beautiful eyes.
Thank you for the small waist and big hips that make me
feel like a Goddess.

Thank you for feet that dance.
Thank you for lips that kiss.
Thank you for the womb that creates.
Thank you for everything you do.

And most importantly,

Thank you for healing.

Thank you for being one of the greatest sources of
wisdom in my life.
My feelings have shifted to self-love.
I honor you.
I love you [exactly as you are.]

Free to Be Divine Love
by Marny Darius

Suriname is a small country in northeastern South America. Covered in tropical rainforests, stunning Dutch colonial-era architecture and showing off one of the most ethnically and culturally diversified populations in the world, Suriname may be small but it is a gem. The Dutch and the British colonized Suriname in the 17ᵗʰ Century and although slavery was abolished in 1863, the practice continued until 1873 when the slaves were finally freed.

This is my personal journey...

Today I honor the abolishment of slavery in Suriname 154 years ago.

I was born in a small village in the interior in Suriname of the Maroon (run away slaves) tribe.

I was raised both in the village and the city. I learned about slavery in school, but wasn't taught or shown to have any anger because of it. I did experience discrimination because of my skin color and where I came from.

Growing up it was hard to accept this skin color, where I came from, and I didn't like these big lips. I wanted to be what I saw on TV, straightening my hair and changing how I dressed. It was part of this journey to seek who I truly was.

I was fortunate to be taught by my grandparents to get an education and work hard to become accomplished.

I've always been a free spirit, wanted to experience so much and didn't let anyone tell me that I couldn't do something. Yep, that's still me.

I saw the world very different than most people; I saw limitless opportunities. In spite of the challenges I faced I saw greatness.

Freedom to be starts within yourself.

I came to America and pursued everything I wanted. I got a good education and placed myself in a well accomplished Caucasian community. Later I owned two businesses and I was successful. I learned so much about myself from the clients who visited the Wellness Spa.
I carried myself as an ambitious, driven, passionate individual with positive energy, not as a single mother of color (even though there is nothing wrong with a single mother of color; it's just a label).
I believe however you feel or whatever you believe of yourself determines how far and where you are in life. I

can only speak from my experience.

I now accept this body, skin color, and where I come from.

I take care of this body, because it is a temple to the most profound part of my being...a beautiful soul/manifestation of Source here to experience Divine Love.

I dress, wear this hair or makeup because of the Divine feminine creative power within, not because of an identity or what society portraits.

I am grateful for and honor what my ancestors went through, the effort they made through so much suffering so that I can freely experience life.

I believe they were driven by something far more powerful and deeper than just freedom of slavery. They were driven by the free will and right of every human being to be free to be Divine Love.

I am here to be Divine Love and not be limited by race, skin color, or social identity.

Love and Light,

Marny

It's All About Me
by Zayna de Gaia

"I can't stand him."
"I hate him."
"What a JERK!"

I repeatedly have said things like that throughout my life. In fact, this was how I'd talk about the person I said I 'loved.'

It was always men: my dad, my brother, or my boyfriend. I didn't say these things out loud; instead, I said them silently, in my own head. Perhaps you could call it an anger problem. Others would blame it on the lack of communication or the stifling silence. Some would say fear was the culprit. I, however, was clear this was a very obvious case of a very, very low level of self-love.

Wait a minute, you're probably asking, what the heck is going on with this story? First the title: It's All About Me. That sounds like something a selfish, self-centered person would say right?

Wrong. In this case, we're talking about someone who is empowered and totally owning her shit. She is saying: I will not point a finger at anyone or anything. This whole thing right here, this whole entire thing, its ALL ABOUT ME. I am 100% responsible for my life. And that's what's up, cause I say so.

That is the new foundation of my life.

Read these lyrics very slowly and carefully; they're from a song I wrote:

> *You're all so fake, sitting on your throne*
> *Looking high and mighty, but you're all alone*
> *When you feel pain, you know I feel it too.*
> *Cause the light inside of me, is the light inside of*
you.

> *Yeah, the silence inside brings many to tears,*
> *And the chaos outside – it ignites the fear.*
> *See, if I call you a hater, then I'm a hater too.*

*And if I say that I'm a lover, then you can be a
lover too.*

Re-read the two last lines.

*See, if I call you a hater, then I'm a hater too.
And if I say that I'm a lover, then you can be a
lover too.*

Our own unwillingness to be with certain aspects of
ourselves creates a resistance to these same aspects
we find in others. For example, if we can't stand it
when people don't keep their word, surely we haven't
reconciled that particular thing for ourselves. Or you
may have a pet peeve about people being late when
they are scheduled to meet with you. So every time
someone is late, you are annoyed and you lose that
loving space. Here's the cool thing: if you can be
alright with that you are a human being and you too
are late sometimes (even if you're super punctual), and
sometimes you may keep your word, and other times,
you may not. If you can be non-judgmental towards
yourself, that's the key to having peace with others.

The extent of which I am willing to not judge myself for
my humanity- is the extent at which I can allow others
to do the same.

What's love got to do with it?

I have learned through my intimate relationships that
every time I complain about something HE'S doing,
you can be assured I am doing the same things
somewhere in my life. And when I learn to love that
part of me, I cease to be the complaining, ungrateful
person that kills off my loving relationships.

Loving myself became about much more than just
giving myself mani-pedis or hot baths. It became about

honoring the pretty and the ugly within me- and when I do this, I can have room for my lover and anyone else to show up as he shows up, with no judgments, just love and room for growth and all the shit that come with that growth.

Yeah, I'm ready for this. I'm ready to love. I'm ready to be loved.

Fully and divinely.

Because I choose to love me first.

Blinded By Consciousness

by Emily Sunset Martinez

It all started with a look, and nothing would be the same.

Once I came into contact with what I wanted, I knew that it would change the very DNA of me. You see, we are all conscious, but blinded. I was walking around life with fabulous sunglasses and a playlist to die for. I was always looking outside myself for that love and attention. Then one day it hit me – it hit me so fucking hard – that if I didn't listen to my intuition I wouldn't be here connecting with you.

You see that is how my life has always been. I would see what society and others wanted for me instead of what I wanted for myself. I would be blinded by the illusions created and have to learn painful lessons. I did learn. I'm the analytic type, looking for the deeper meaning, and lessons. I crave living life to the fullest. The problems would arise when I would choose the easy road.

I chose the easy road until one day my body said "no more" and pulled the brakes. My body was signaling the white flag of "no more pain." At that moment I choose to take the blinders off and not give up on me. I decided to jump off the cliff and go back to basics.

I came to this cliff in my senior year of high school. I was in a relationship that I didn't want, had a dysfunctional family, and was diagnosed with anxiety, bipolar, and depression all at once.

I knew that if I did not take the necessary risk then I would keep going down this path to a tasteless life. I knew I had to stop hiding behind my old story and just be me.

So when I was asked this question, "do you love yourself?" It was hard because to a certain degree I've always loved myself. But I only paid attention to surface parts of me, not realizing how deep my waters really run.

I truly chose to love myself when I let go of the idea of "control."

I chose to love myself when I felt in my heart the pain I had created and knew it was time to rip the Band-Aid off.

I chose to love myself when my battle scars weren't appreciated.

I chose to love myself when I wanted to be happy and stop waiting around for the perfect moment, place, or person.

I chose to love myself when I heard the cries of my brothers and sisters so loud that I couldn't sleep at night.

I chose to love myself when I saw her ingest the poison of envy and pain.

I chose to love myself when we let our ego get in the way.

I chose to love myself when I saw the monster stare back at me with fear so loud it hit me in the soul.

I chose to love myself when I knew that the devil didn't only take ten percent.

I chose to love myself when the aches inside of me said "no more."

I chose to love myself when she lay there and no one helped, not even a cop.

I chose to love myself when the fishes kissed the fear away. I chose to love myself when I let his words kill the illusions.

I chose to love myself when I danced away the pain.

I chose to love myself when I tried to speak, but there were not words to say.

I chose to love myself when I closed my eyes and the bliss sizzled my skin like the fire.

I chose to love myself when I knew there was another way.

I'm still on the road to self-love. I may not listen to myself all the time, but building awareness has its own flow. What gets in the way for me are the negative voices. The voices that say I'm not smart enough, interesting or cool enough, or I become judgmental and mean. Those are the voices that keep me so far away from the real me. It's almost like I'm there looking at myself and every time I go to say something one of those voices comes and clogs my ears.

So what do you do when you have a whole lot of trash to clean up with yourself and so little time? I would break down and blame the world because I didn't have a voice to explain the transitions that were happening in my life. I don't know how to deal with the things that I did but was never aware of.

What I know is that I may not have all the answers to everything, but I am aware of what I'm doing and what I have gained. That is what I have always been doing, but never aware of. I was aware of all the pain in my life because I know I put it there, but now I want to plant love in my heart.

Sticking to my essence and choosing me will always guide me on the road to cleaning up and transforming all at the same time. When I stop analyzing the moment and start just being with it, I live more. I connect with myself on a deeper level because I feel what emotions and sensations come up and see if they are in line with who I am. I've taken responsibility for what I say and relate that to how I feel. No more putting my life in someone else's hands.

Breathing.

Even just writing the word helps.

I remind myself to breathe all the time. I write it on my hand, on my notebooks — everywhere. If you don't breathe you will drive yourself mad and miss out on your life. When I feel that pressure on my chest or stomach, I breathe right into that area. I breathe deep because once it spreads I lose touch with myself and in that moment and I become a machine.

Being in my own rawness delights my soul, down to the very depth of me.

And I don't need the sunglasses.

The Girl With the Love Within
by Karina Rosado

I am hurt...

Those are the first words that came to mind as I decided to write this piece. I feel pain, sorrow, agony, and just a plain old discomfort. Like most people, I will tell you I have been through a lot. My journey has taken me so deep into my soul that sometimes I wonder, why did all of this happen to me?

I will start by saying that the first time I asked why, I was seven years old. I was getting ready to go to school like any normal day, but I had no idea that I was about to go through a life changing moment that would mark the awakening of my consciousness and myself forever.

I got hit by a car on my way to school.

I woke up on the floor with my aunt asking me if I was okay, and a bunch of paramedics all around me. I was hit right when I started to cross the street on this wide road and I never saw it coming. I don't remember a thing. I just remember getting a little bit off the cemented sidewalk to see if there were any cars coming, and that was that. Then I woke up feeling almost paralyzed from my legs down. I had broken both of my legs: the top bones of both of my thighs. I was rushed to the hospital where they took x-ray after x-ray, and then I was hospitalized for about a month and a half to two months.

Every day I had to keep my legs straight in this sling, and eat hospital food, which I never really complained about. In fact, I remember feeling a rare sense of comfort, as I knew that I was inevitably and instinctively going to be taken care of no matter what. You see, as a child I was raised by my grandmother. She showed up every day at the hospital to bring me home cooked meals and hang out with me for most of the day. She was my guardian angel who never let me down, and she always seemed to know what I needed.

But I continued to feel baffled by the idea that kept creeping into my mind, why did this happen to me? Why me, I would say, why me?

My father then showed up to take care of me and he came every day for the remainder of my stay at the hospital, and also stayed with me as I was released and nurtured me until his departure. My father lived in the Dominican Republic and had separated from my mom when I was very young. He suffered from bipolar disorder and would have these violent episodes where he wanted to throw me off the bed.

My mother on the other hand suffered from her own sense of psychological turmoil. When she gave birth to her first daughter, who was born dead without a neck or a throat, my mother suffered tremendously though all of that. She proceeded to have my brother and I and throughout her pregnancies – and even after she gave birth – she suffered from a form of postpartum depression and hallucinations.

There was a Dominican tall tale that would say if you washed your hair after you gave birth you would go crazy. So my mother believed all of that in her subconscious, and when she decided to wash her hair one day, she was never able to live in peace again. She felt as if she was losing it. She was very sensitive as a child, raised asthmatic in the mountains of Dominican Republic and perhaps misunderstood most of her life.

She was very different from the rest, in that she was a very gentle and sensitive being, and in our culture it was looked down upon to be that way. You had to be a strong, independent, go-getter, and my mother was all of those things but in her own way. She was a child of God who came to earth to perhaps teach others about compassion and self-love. She rarely ever complained as people criticized her and ridiculed her and put her down. I can see now so very well how her story mirrors a bit of my own.

As the years passed by, my mother separated from my dad, lived with my grandmother for some time, and then remarried another man, the father of her three children. My father also went his separate way, had a few affairs, and eventually married another woman with whom he had three other children as well.

I, on the other hand, remained living with my grandmother as I was told I became very attached to her as a baby and a child and did not want to leave when my mother left with her new husband. Some years passed by, I had the accident, I recovered from that slowly but surely, but I remember feeling hurt that my mom and dad were not together. I also remember feeling physical pain in my hips for some time every time I bent over or stood up too fast from the accident.

I witnessed how my family rejected my mother's new husband, as he was a tough cookie. Somehow he too judged my mother for her condition, and would kick her out of her own home at times. Sometimes he would drop off his kids at my grandmother's house, at times with no shoes on, grumble a few words and then take off. It was so bizarre to witness all of this, because I felt he too was misunderstood. Nobody liked him in the family, he was never part of any family affairs, and he seemed to be a negative, unhappy and an abusive person. I remember the few encounters that I had with him were always him trying to hit my brother and I, and I would rebel completely against him. I never felt happy with this guy. Never.

My mother continued to live with him in what seemed sheer and utter poverty. They always had food in the fridge, but it was never a nice, loving, warm and inviting home. It was always a home he was constructing, where everything seemed broken or unable to be used, and where there was a lack of continuity and consistency.

My mother was always in bed, and when she regained her strength she would use that little bit of energy to cook, and take care of her three children. Sometimes these kids were jumping off the walls. They had no real discipline, and grew up with their parents never really showing a sense of unity. Broken walls, a dirty home, and a sense of unhappiness hung in the air. It remained like this for most of their lives, until their adulthood.

As I became an adult, I went through my own ups and downs. I was raised by my grandmother until the age of fourteen. At that time she had decided to move to the Dominican Republic, where she bought a house with her son and his wife and I had decided I did not want to go live there. I wanted to stay in the United States. Which led me to live with my mother for the first time since I was a kid.

My grandmother died four years later from lung cancer and never got to live her dream and live in her country. She was diagnosed with cancer shortly after she had decided to move and she never got to go. I witnessed her slowly decompose and become unrecognizable, as the years passed by. She died in 1998, four months after I graduated high school.

I cried so hard when she passed away. More than I have ever cried before. It was painful to watch this beautiful, wonderful, strong woman, who had been my rock for most of my life, just pass away in such a horrible way. I loved her very deeply, and admired her tenacity, and her ability to always keep everything and everyone together. I was her deep love, and she was mine as well. The road in our relationship wasn't always that rosy, but for the most part it was heaven, because we both shared this inseparable bond and communion together. She raised me to be a Queen Bee, and she somehow gave me the foundation that I needed to make it on my own.

Before she passed away, I ended up living with my brother in an apartment, which was three of four blocks away from my mother's home in Massachusetts. Somehow my mother was able to get on Section 8 and my brother and I moved in.

We were never able to get along with her husband and for the first time we were all living under the same roof. My brother, who was raised by my dad for most of his life, I who was raised by my grandmother for most of my life, and suddenly we were all breathing the same air, under the same roof, with my mother, her husband, and my other three siblings.

At times things were cool, because I had started a new life, met new friends, and spent a lot of my time at school and or working to earn a living. My brother was somewhat of a jock, had already established relationships with people there, so when I came into the picture, the foundation was already set. I just had to live in it.

But there were still moments of hardship while living in the turmoil of my mother's life. I remember having to take care of myself from day one. Always being on the lookout for me and myself. Building a relationship with myself and my heart. Always taking care of me. I made most of my life decisions on my own. Like where to work as a teenager, financing my first car, getting into college, traveling to New York to work during the summers, buying my own clothes and school supplies, even going to the doctors. I did it all. I was my mother and my father in one.

I have to admit, I made these really good friends that would come to my rescue when I was in a funk. I would get really depressed from time to time and felt really unhappy, but my friends Ana and Indhira would come to my rescue and take me out to the movies; we would travel to New York together and party quite a bit as I got a little older. They were there to help me through and gave me unconditional support.

College was fun; again I was in charge of picking my major, paying for school, and preparing myself for a better future. But as I recall, looking back at the craziness of my mother's life and her husband's tumultuous relationship, left me fending for myself.

From the age of 14 and on I was raised in a somewhat dysfunctional and hostile environment – where anger and negativity was felt in the air so often that as the emotional destruction continued, pain started to swell in my soul again. Which really resembles depression at the end. I would go to school and feel depressed at times, and the worst part about it was that I would say something to some of my friends, but they made me feel like there was something wrong with me. I feel like to this day. It is hard for me to open up about my true feelings with people, because whatever I was feeling in the past was somewhat not validated and instead was put down by others that had no idea of what I was going through.

Eventually and essentially I started to get over it. As high school graduation was fast approaching, a new life was beginning to manifest right before my eyes. I never looked back on all the turmoil I encountered. I only looked forward. Because the harder I worked, the more I was able and capable to rise above and get a better life! What I had gone through propelled me to have the strength and determination to move on and work hard to get to where I wanted. Which was away from craziness and drama, into a normal home with a successful career and lifestyle.

The summer of 2001 I went through a very difficult heartbreak with my first love, and then ended up getting into an abusive long distance relationship with one of my coworkers. I lived in Massachusetts and he lived in North Carolina. He seemed very charming to most people, but behind closed doors he was a different person. Always moody, and unhappy it seemed. At times I would go visit him in his home where he kept a rifle underneath his bed, and I swear to you, there were moments I felt like this guy could have been one of those men that would kill his girlfriend when asleep or something. I don't know that he would ever do that, but instinctively I felt that way. I was scared of him and I didn't know it.

As time elapsed I continued on with this relationship until one day I had a heart to heart conversation with another coworker who told me that she was in an abusive relationship. She explained to me that what I was going through seemed like the beginning of one, and to get out of it while I could. Since her husband would drag her down the stairs by the hair in the midst of their heavy arguments, she would resort to drinking as a way to calm herself down.

I told her my boyfriend would call me in the middle of the night drunk, and would say, your voice sounds clear, who are you Fuck*** . He kicked me off the bed one time, and because of his jealousy and possessiveness would call incessantly to see what I was doing, when I was away on vacation. As my coworker and I continued to confide with each other, we became good friends, and she lit the proverbial match in the dark tunnel that I was traveling in with this guy. He was possessive, verbally abusive, and he probably was borderline alcoholic. He just wasn't right.

After three years of being together I prayed to God and I asked him for a way out, as there were moments where I was having nightmares of us getting married, or trying to at least, and I would literally run out the altar, because I didn't want to be with him like that. So my prayer was answered, and a few months later, I realized that this guy seemed to have girlfriends all around the states. He was lying to me, and was cheating on me with other women. So I broke it off with him and never saw him again. He even stole fifteen hundred dollars from me at that time as well. So that was his ticket out the door.

A few months later I met the man that would change my life

forever. The father of my child, and now my second child. Again I asked God, to help me manifest a relationship where I would experience the great joy of having great sex, as I could never climax with my ex and at times he seemed to want it more than I did, but I wasn't happy with him, or our sex life for that matter.

So here I go again, calling in the universe for something that I wanted and needed to experience. And here came this charming, kind of bad boy guy, with whom I experienced the best sex I have ever had, but yet, I also experienced the most sorrow. By that time I had moved out of the apartment I shared with my brother. My mother moved in with me, and eventually we decided to move to a different place. We lived together for some time and we moved yet again to a not so good neighborhood in the town where I grew up in. My uncle rented us an apartment there for very cheap, but we had to deal with cockroaches and loud crazy neighbors, and not to mention as time progressed, I started to feel these weird sensations while living there as well.

I started my initial spiritual awakening there, only to primarily experience dark energies around me, and I would see glimpses of what seemed like lost spirits or ghosts at night. It was quite the scary and frightening experience. There was a moment where I felt a spirit in my body and it suddenly came out of me. Everything was just so weird. I was uneasy with these new experiences and started to feel super sensitive. I honestly did not understand what was happening to me at that moment; all I felt was fright and nervousness, and a sense of depression would come over me.

Although I was going through these energetic changes, I still managed to have fun, go out drinking and partying with my cousins and friends, but there came a point where

I experienced a change in my body. Suddenly I could not process alcohol as well; my body started to reject it and I would shake the next day after I drank. I felt nervous a lot too, and I noticed I just could not handle certain things the same way anymore. My body was becoming this sensitive, energy vessel where I could see and feel energy.

Suddenly with no warning it just started to happen. The first time I experienced this sensation of sensing things, especially bad things, was when I was introduced to my best friend's friend, the girl we moved in with after my brother and I had to leave our first apartment.

She eventually moved out with her, since she and my brother had a big fall out, and she did not get along with him or his wife. A time came where I moved out of that "crazy apartment" I lived in with my mother and into my own place. My mother went back to live with her husband because my sister got pregnant and I could no longer continue to sustain a household, while working full time and going to school, and also taking care of my mother, my sister and her newborn. My sister did not cooperate with paying bills, and my mother did not cook for me as often as I wanted to and or needed since I was already doing so much and practically was surviving on very low fuel.

Perhaps that is what led me to join what I know now to be a cult. Because at some point all of the craziness gets to you. All of the drama, the pain, the hurt, and the judgments breaks you down, and make you run for your life, run as fast as you can, away from it all.

I don't remember exactly when this happened, but I started having out of body experiences. It was when I moved into my new apartment by myself. I was living on the second floor of my aunt's house and I remember visiting a therapist because I started to feel like I would leave my body, look very scared and alone, and then I would come back in. I ended up looking for refuge in this yoga center, subconsciously, not because of my out of body experiences, but because ironically I was looking for a way to relieve stress and take a break from school. I had been going through so much that I decided I needed some time off to regroup, and find myself again.

I got really involved with this yoga practice, became part of it and eventually moved in with all of the yoga masters that taught. I started teaching yoga, and I invested all of my life savings into the trainings. I did not realize it was a cult until it was too late and I felt like I needed to get out, but by that time I had to finish what I started because had I left beforehand I would've been completely lost and distraught from all that I had become. It was like hatching an egg before its time.

I had to be indoctrinated to truly learn the ins and outs of what I would call my own spirituality at that point. I always knew that I would not stay there, but I could not leave. There I learned to teach energy yoga and heal people. I became very acute and aware of people's bodily dysfunctions, emotions, thoughts and feelings. I felt everything. The more I taught, and the more healings I received, the more I could feel life itself unfold right in front of my eyes through people. They taught me how I was very good at what I did but I can also sense how people could hold pain in different parts of their bodies. It was just a very interesting endeavor and super life changing.

I was very young at that point so I was susceptible to everything. I was learning all of these spiritual principals, while feeling hurt and depressed because I was changing so much and I was not readily allowed to visit family members or involve them in what I was going through. It's funny though, because beyond all the change that I was experiencing, and the transformation I was undergoing, I still felt a sense of love and support from the Universe at that time. I learned from an early age to have a connection to self, perhaps because of my grandmother and the support she held throughout the years as I was growing up. She helped me to learn how to be independent, think for myself, and take appropriate action when needed.

And although my vision of self was somewhat muddled, because so much of me was used to living an earthly life, all of a sudden I entered a place where you kind of left your identity behind to become "A spiritual Being." I still felt that deep inner connection to myself and proceeded to live in accordance with that feeling. The feeling that I was not alone, and that even though I was hurting, I still loved myself. It's almost as if my upbringing and the way I was raised, helped me keep it together, and hold everything in place. I was very mature in the sense that, although it was difficult to change so much, especially in contrast to a society that celebrated everything negative (at least the one I lived in) and were very judgmental, I knew that God had a higher purpose for me there, and that in no time I would leave, and the lessons continued to pour in after my departure.

After I left the cult I got ridiculed a lot by people, they judged me, put me down, talked about me and put me in the worst category there was to put anyone... Perhaps because I mirrored myself as a sensitive, young, and unable-to-defend-myself kind of person. This is where I feel like my story resembles my mother's story. She married a guy nobody liked and he was not allowed anywhere close to family premises, she was sick and sensitive and probably was experiencing her own spiritual awakening but was being judged and ridiculed through it all. She had hallucinations, and was put down at the end of the barrel. Same thing happened to me.

I was in a relationship where my family strongly disapproved of my husband. He had a bad reputation in their eyes and also was a drug addict at that time. He resorted to cocaine and alcohol as his drug of choice, to help heal and cope with his own past. I was super sensitive after leaving the cult; I got pregnant shortly after and had to go through a pregnancy full of depression, pain and sorrow.

I always wanted to be in a happy relationship, a happy marriage. It would break my heart to witness the man that I loved, and still love, go through all of this and almost die in my arms, because at times he almost overdosed.

I gave birth to a beautiful baby boy, but never felt true and real joy after that. I lived in places where I did not want to be. In a town where everybody knew each other and gossiped about each other's lives. In a town where arrogance was accompanied by ignorance and intolerance towards anything humble, good, and compassionate. I gained 60 pounds, and developed hypothyroidism, along with anemia, and low blood sugar. I was so depressed I didn't want to eat. I felt unable to proceed in life, and uncertain where to go... My husband at times could not afford the rent, so there were many times where I was homeless, had little to nothing to eat, and no matter how hard I tried to move on, I was just so down and out I could not gather the energy, inspiration, and motivation to move forward. I had changed so much, and evolved my consciousness so much, that it was hard for me to live a normal day to day life, working a 9 to 5 job.

There came a time I felt so sick, I almost felt like I was dying, like my body was giving up on me. There were moments where I would spend hours on end healing myself energetically day after day, until I felt instinctively like I was done. People like family and friends felt bad for me I suppose. But to me it came across as a form of judgment.

I had lost all of my money, my reputation, my looks, my stamina; I lost it all. And there were herds of people coming around to say, "Look at you now." Rather than being supportive and loving towards me, they were rude and condescending. It took a lot for me to heal from all of that.

I had to move away from all of that negativity to a place that was more productive... As a matter of fact, I moved around quite a bit for some time. Some people were there for me, but a lot of them closed their doors. I realized who my real true friends were. Which essentially were my mother and my husband's mother at that time.

Those were the only two that never judged and were there to hold us through everything.

Through all of these emotional rollercoasters, growing up I always felt this sense of deep love, and presence coming through me and within me. I learned from an early age to develop this relationship with myself where I would find nourishment in my heart. I felt it a lot throughout the first half of my life because I had my grandmother as my foundation and rock and she showed me what it is to be there for one self. By her being there for me, it instilled in me a deep sense of respect and admiration for myself. I feel as if her soul was there to teach me that lesson. That no matter what happens, I can always count on myself.

To be quite honest, I really don't know how she did it, but

whoever she was and still is, she came to my life to give me a deep sense of fresh air, and I know that even after she passed away she continued to whisper her love and her appreciation to me through thick and thin, although there were moments where I could not feel that love because I experienced quite the opposite coming from other people.

The second half of my life became so hard that I might have lost that connection with myself for a bit. But I realize now, that love is never lost, it is just forgotten. As I fended for my life, in a state of pure and primal survival, feeling ashamed for what I had become, or worse yet what people dictated I had become, not having enough money to even look the part, I realized that as vain as this may sound, they were things I felt I had before that defined me.

I learned the hard way that looks, money, reputation, and accumulation of wealth does not define who I am as a person. I always knew that inherently, but the people around me felt differently. Their egos were stronger than their hearts, and it showed, and I followed and fell into that trap. Because if so many people say there is something wrong with you, you eventually start to believe it.

I had to be presented with situations and people time and time again that would put me down, to help me realize that I am more than my looks, more than the car I drive, the house I live in, the person that I date, the reputation I uphold, even the education that I have; I am so much more than that! I developed deep and true compassion for myself and others. I loved me deeply but I loved others at times even more. I felt other's pain and sorrow and at times I wanted to heal them so badly, because I knew exactly the pain they were going through. I wanted to help, but there were moments that I forgot about myself again.

I forgot to love me back. I asked that from others, when in reality I needed to give that to myself as well. Day in and day out, I am reminded of this lesson.

To truly blossom in this life, you have to put yourself first, and build a relationship with your higher self and God for that matter. Because they are always there waiting for you to recognize them and accept them into your life. They don't judge, don't ridicule. They just love, accept and love again. And because of this connection I learned to have from an early age, I was able to undergo the worst of all experiences, and still come out of it alive. So with that said....

Love yourself, for no one else will as much as you can. No matter what you are going through. You will get through it.

For if I did, you can too.

爱
LETTING GO

Living Guilt Free

by Leilla Blackwell

GUILT: a painful feeling of self-reproach resulting from a belief that one has done something wrong or immoral.[1]

I know guilt. I understand it. I know how to use it. It is not a foreign concept to me. I have tried it on and even worn it a few times. That's how I know it's not a natural fit for me at this stage in my life.

I think after the age of twelve, guilt is a useless feeling. I can feel guilt, but it's not my natural tendency. I have embraced my more authentic source of conscience and self-discipline, empathy. When I stopped placating others by wasting time and energy manufacturing feelings of guilt, I was able to maximize the expression of my empathic nature and discipline myself and others through love and acceptance, not guilt and blame.

$$Conscience = Guilt + Empathy$$
$$Guilt = Me \text{ vs. } You$$
$$Empathy = You \text{ \& } Me$$

My guilt button is broken, and you can break yours too.

Conscience is formed through early life experiences that pair guilt and empathy. You do something that causes an undesirable consequence that affects someone else. The adults in your life point out to you that the other person has been hurt by something you did.

They do this to teach you to be responsible for your actions, considerate of others, and mindful that your actions create consequences that extend beyond you as an individual.

This is a healthy dynamic. Unfortunately, it rarely stays this way. Punishment gets introduced as a tool to cement this concept. At some point we shift from taking responsibility for our actions, to internalizing what we do as who we are. We stack these experiences and add them up to mean that we are wrong, that we are flawed and worthy of punishment, not love. We focus on punishing ourselves as we get older and our parents aren't punishing us anymore.

My conscience is driven by empathy. My father was violent with a personality disorder and my mother had narcissistic tendencies (her survival mechanism). If I could accurately intuit the needs of my parents and meet those needs in meaningful ways, I would be safe from their anger as well as safe from experiencing their personal pain, which was even more difficult for me than dealing with my own.

The emotional pain of others is painful to me and I avoid being the source of that pain. If I inadvertently hurt someone or even make him or her uncomfortable, I feel hurt because they feel hurt. I don't want them or me to feel that way, but I don't feel like I am bad or wrong. Sometimes things happen that are undesirable and I'm just as human as anyone, so I make mistakes, and I ask myself, "how can I help make it right or at least better?" I am simultaneously kind to myself and the other person by responding with love.

THE BONDAGE OF GUILT AND BLAME

Growing up, I was punished whether I did something wrong or not. It was safer to use me as a scapegoat because I was a child and the consequences might be less severe for me, so I accepted the blame whether I was responsible or not. I didn't form a connection with guilt, since the blame wasn't based in reality. I make choices based on what is right, not in avoidance of feelings of guilt.

I am uncomfortable with others who carry a lot of guilt, because I see guilt as selfish – self-protective, as in "don't hurt me back, see I'm already hurting, I'm already punishing me, there's nothing left for you to do to me to make this right." If you have done something that caused pain or discomfort in someone else, your primary focus is more appropriately placed on helping the other person feel better for them, not assuaging your own guilty feelings. That would be like hitting someone with your car and crying on his or her shoulder at the hospital because you feel terrible about what you did – it doesn't fit.

Having an empathic nature without guilt means I don't blame –no self-blame and no blame of others. I have been asked multiple times, "Where does the blame go?" I almost don't understand this question, but it comes up often enough that it must be a real question. The only answer I have is, there is no place for blame, and so it doesn't have anywhere appropriate to go.

Any time you use blame, you are trying to manipulate someone into being responsible for your experience of your life circumstance. They can only be held responsible for their experience. So you can kindly show them how they are contributing to creating an experience outside of their nature, if that's true for them; and if it's not, why would you expect them to behave outside of their nature for you? You can express to them how their actions impacted you and ask for what you need them to provide as reparation, without expectation that your need will be satisfied by them. "I'm confused by what just happened. You are usually so thoughtful. I'm disappointed that ... Do you think you could ...?" – Which is very different from, "I can't believe you did... Because of you, now... You should..."

Along with no blame, I "forgive" easily. It's not really "forgiving" because I don't actually blame, but I do let others off the hook easily and am very accepting of others however they come, I don't judge. I am able to love easily and deeply.

I recognize that we all have strengths and weaknesses. I don't count on others to achieve excellence in their areas of weakness. It's not productive or helpful to hold someone accountable in the moment for something they didn't have the capacity to do differently.

This can be a blessing and a curse. I had to learn how to discipline myself and others through love, or easily be taken advantage of repeatedly while never holding the other person responsible for their actions. I had to get connected with what it feels like to filter my responses through love– which is mutually beneficial and unconditional–instead of fear, which is narrow and conditional.

Even with traumatic experiences, I don't place blame on myself or the perpetrator of the offense(s). The experience is a learning opportunity for me and them, if they choose to learn anything from it. I simply see it for what it is, that it contributed to who I am, and I love who I am today.

Every day opportunities are presented to me to discipline through love. Personal temptations can be dismissed by choosing the most loving choice. Fear, worry, and anger can readily dissipate when actions and reactions are filtered through love. I can release someone's anger of me, if I know I did the best I could do in the moment. If I choose love first, I can move through challenges in life without the distractions of resentment or revenge.

I do not believe in punishment. Even in extreme circumstances, prison is the tool used as an appropriate consequence, not for punishment. We offer boundaries and consequences for children until they develop self-control. If they don't develop self-control, then the law controls them and police officers are charged with delivering that control, while the courts enforce it through imprisonment. Energetically, if you are violent and malevolent, then you need to live where violence and malevolence lives – in prison.

Discipline through love is always kind, but not always gentle. When you love someone (including yourself), you don't contribute to them degrading their nature by supporting them in destructive (hence self-destructive) choices; including abusive behavior, whether emotionally or physically abusive. So in loving them you support them in being their best self while diverting them from degrading their nature by lovingly disciplining the relationship. Therefore you don't accept mistreatment as part of your reality. When you practice BEING FULLY OPEN IN LOVE, you perfect your self-expression and your self-knowledge so you know and understand what is truly an expression of your highest self and what is ego driven.

FREEDOM IN COMPASSION, SURRENDER AND PLEASURE

Suicide has pervaded my life since I was a child. While I have not been suicidal, these thoughts have infected the minds of a few of my very close loved ones. It is very painful to witness someone you love suffer; the fear and desperation are crippling to them and those who love them. It's very easy to go into "fix it" mode, but I have learned true compassion by working through some of these very extreme feelings.

My first experience was with my father. He tried to hang himself when my mother left him. I woke up to find him standing on a chair with the noose around his neck, staring blankly with tears rolling down his cheeks. I cried, I yelled, I begged, I screamed at him. I was nine years old; I didn't know what to do. I had enough experience with violence and trauma in my home that asking for help wasn't a consideration.

He just stared and cried, quietly mumbling to himself. I caught a few familiar words in his mumbling and realized he was praying the same prayer over and over again, his favorite prayer, Psalm 23. He taught me that prayer and said it with me at bedtimes. So I said it with him "... I shall not want... restoreth my soul... yea though I walk through the valley of the shadow of death... I shall fear no evil... for thou art with me... comfort me... goodness and mercy shall follow me..."

At some point it became my prayer, for me. I began to draw strength from those words and the spirit in them. I had less desperation and fear. I was walking through the valley of the shadow of death. I found comfort. I felt goodness and mercy. Then my father saw me; he always could see me, he just wouldn't. He saw me crying, I begged him again to come down and eventually he did. I developed compassion for me and then he could feel the compassion for him and be open to it.

The main lesson for me has been to stop resisting it and just be with it. We often think we need to convince a person suffering, that their pain isn't worthy of death. How do we know it's not? Instead of resisting the death, work with the person, unify, to kill the pain. You don't have to agree that they should kill themselves in order to acknowledge that their suffering may be unbearable. Get on their side, form an army of two or more to do battle against their suffering. That doesn't mean you must fix it, it may not be fixable, even by them. But being with them through it is powerful. Life transitions, although a natural, healthy and necessary part of life, can be painful. A person in pain often cannot see past the pain. Don't judge their suffering, see them, and witness their growth and growing pains. Walk through the fire with them, or at least hold their hand.

The death of Robin Williams and how it was handled by the mainstream media and in social media is a prime example. Having compassion would mean that we have to put aside ourselves and our judgments of someone else's life and choices. Acknowledge that they may suffer in ways that are unimaginable to us. Someone suffering with mental illness is hardly more in control of the outcome of that disease, than someone with cancer. Yet when depression or mental illness wins the fight, we judge the person, instead of having compassion and understanding that perhaps they made the most loving choice that they were capable of at the time. In the end, they die from their illness just the same. It is sad and tragic, but not worthy of judgment.

Find acceptance and compassion, even when you can't come to a place of understanding. You unbind your heart from the suffering that distracts you from love.

I'M A GIVER!

Part of human nature is being giving. As women, it's easy for us to overdevelop this giving muscle. We give of ourselves until there is nothing left. We don't just leave ourselves empty; we disappear, we become lost, so even the container is void. If we are not giving, we don't know how to relate, what role to play in an interaction; we literally feel lost.

If you're not being a giver, what are you being? ... A taker?
No, you are a receiver.

You are open, receptive, and when you take in the gifts of
life, the gifts that others have offered up to you, life is
pleased to be received, others are pleased to have their gifts
accepted and valued, you are pleased. In receiving pleasure,
you are simultaneously a source of pleasure; in the
experience of it, it is experienced. If you grow to know the
beauty–the bounty–of receiving, you will not feel guilt or
fear surrounding taking; you will become gifted at receiving.

Imagine you could find your pleasure in making the one
you love feel like the most rare and precious gem at the end
of the day. You spend your time discovering and
rediscovering how each facet of that person shines as you
polish and make them sparkle with your love and attention.
What effect can you have on them?

Imagine you are free to love. What if that person is YOU?
You become radiant and glowing with joy, pleasure and
love.

We are all one. Cut from the same cloth, our bodies are
separate, but our essence – our soul – is one divine being.

When I look at you, I see you and I see God in you. When
you look at me, I offer myself to you and I offer the God in
me, to you. There is really no giving and no taking in this
dynamic. This is sharing. Sharing is mutual.

Receiving is tied to surrender; surrender is tied to trust. To
receive we must open, create space, be vulnerable. Then we
must trust that the reward is worth the risk. I consciously
choose to surrender and receive. It's risky for me too. I
consciously choose to trust that the Divine source is at

work and at play when I am presented with an opportunity to receive something bountiful. It is much harder for me to turn God away than it is to turn away a body separate from mine. In looking for the divine in everything, I am practiced at recognizing the divine, that makes trusting and surrender a little easier.

THERE IS PURPOSE IN PLEASURE.

We are taught that being expressive of our feminine nature is an open invitation to abuse or being taken advantage of. Outside of the bedroom or nursery, being feminine, is often perceived as inappropriate.

Throughout our 25 years plus together (and three children), my husband has taught me a lot about the beauty in a man's nature and about myself as a woman, freeing me of the fear and negative associations with my own nature, affording me the pleasure of love, real love that comes from an abundance of love that fills me to overflowing from the inside, which drew me into learning more about the dynamics between men and women. Witnessing the patterns has been very freeing to me. I no longer feel guilty about my feminine self-expression.

I am blessed with a feminine spirit that includes dynamic sensual energy and an openly loving essence. Even as a child, I radiated this vibrational energy. I love dancing and music, enjoy beauty, am affectionate, playful and laugh easily, can be eager to please, cooperative, kind and gentle.

I used to view my nature as a curse, not a blessing. While I gravitated to others who were like me, I also attracted the opposite; the users, abusers, those looking for someone to take advantage of, those who wanted to corrupt. Open and loving was interpreted as gullible and easy, while a dynamic sensual nature was perceived as sexually available. I was aware of needing to hide my nature and make myself invisible by the age of nine because of the severity of the blatant inappropriate attention I often found myself on the receiving end of.

Then a teacher made sexual advances toward me. He was someone I thought I could trust, someone I believed I could count on to see me and know that I was worthy of his protection, not his perversion. For over a year he treated me like a real person, a student that he valued, until the day his hand slid up my thigh when I was twelve. My immediate response was rage. I was so angry that I had allowed myself to believe that another human could see something in me worthy of being cherished. I was enraged at the proof that someone that I valued couldn't find value in me; the only value to be had was sex with me. My anger shocked both of us in that moment and he left without hurting me physically, but my spirit was wounded. I never saw him again.

When I told an adult about it, their response confirmed that I was responsible for what happened; I should have known better than to believe that a man could have any interest in me beyond sex, since I didn't have anything else to offer him. Here am I, the idiot, believing that at twelve-years-old sex was the one thing I didn't have to offer an adult man. I knew this wasn't right, it didn't feel right to me. But I didn't know what else to do to stay safe other than to take responsibility for myself, especially when the adults in my life were the ones taking advantage of me, or were overburdened by the responsibility of protecting me. So I protected myself by trying to be responsible for how others saw me. I tried even harder to hide with the clothes I wore; I made myself blank. I didn't look at or engage with people. I built protective walls around myself to block the "bad" people out, but I also largely blocked the good ones out too, and even worse, I locked myself in.

Containing my nature and locking myself away became exhausting, depressing and lonely. Even when I got close to other people, I didn't allow them to get close to me. I started to see that I was frustrating myself and the people who love me. My husband and friends could feel that I was withholding. In unguarded moments they could catch glimpses of me, the real me, free-spirited, enthusiastic, open, and radiant with love. I started to enjoy experiencing my own energy in these moments. I learned to be loved. I grew to accept that I am that woman.

My energy may still be misinterpreted and there might be those who want to pervert and corrupt. But I'm not afraid anymore. I let go of my need to control others by stifling me. I choose to be a source of life, light, love, pleasure, joy and I can't do that if I am playing dead. I no longer feel the need to take responsibility for the feelings of others by hiding my nature. I feel free to be me, the best of me, and I wish for every woman to feel that free flowing love and acceptance for who they are at their core (every person, really).

Feminine energy is the source, keeper, fountain, and well of pleasure.

Stay in touch with the term "source" of pleasure, not to be confused with "object" of pleasure. Being a source of pleasure means that pleasure lives inside you; there's no need to seek it outside yourself. So you don't need to indulge in pleasurable things, in order to access this feeling.

You don't need to get a massage or wear expensive perfumes to experience pleasure. Massages and pleasant scents become an expression or manifestation of the pleasure that flows from you naturally. So you don't waste your precious energy chasing yumminess, because you are yummy, you do yummy things.

You infuse life... yours and those around you ...with deliciousness.

This is the ideal.

We are not all there all the time. So in the pursuit of experiencing pleasure, which is a core component of life and aliveness, we turn to food, sex, alcohol, spa days, scented candles, bubble baths, music and dance, walks in nature, luxurious fabrics and fashion, flowers... even vicarious pleasures like comedy or romantic movies, children and the purity of their spirit and abandon of their laughter.

These types of things are wonderful ways to reconnect with the pleasure that lives inside us. But it's important to engage with them as just that, a way to reconnect, recognize and re-engage with the pleasure we already contain. The trouble comes into play when we use this for pleasure. Imagine lighting scented candles or incense because breathing air that smells sweet is aligned with you, because you are sweetness and therefore breathing sweet air is not an escape from you and your life, it is coming home. Imagine that enjoying childlike laughter and abandon is you, and you can laugh with complete abandon WITH the children and even adults instead of simply being reminded of what that used to be like when you were a child.

As women, we are keepers of the gift of pleasure...

We are a source of pleasure for men, children and even other women. While we are not responsible for the pleasure of others, we are responsible for being good stewards of the gifts we have been graced with. The first step is the awareness that we contain this boundless source of pleasure inside ourselves, wrapped up in our femininity.

If we disengage from our authentic feminine nature, we forget what pleases us; we forget the ways in which we can be pleasing. We become tired, cranky, prickly, needy, bitter, self-centered, and unhealthy. We feel lonely, unloved, depressed, desperate, sick, resentful, angry, and fearful. Our intimate relationships lack intimacy and feel empty, our work interactions are characterized by competition and lack, our friendships are catty and gossipy, our lives seem filled with frustration and struggle – not fulfilling.

We have unhealthy associations with attention, affection, receiving and self-expression; it either feels like too much, or not enough. We are out of flow and out of harmony.

When we are filled to overflowing with love (everyone's gift) and pleasure (unique to the feminine), we feed the feminine spirit of others. Just by being in our presence, they will engage with the feminine and become more aware of the feminine in themselves and access to pleasure. You may make connections by playing with this energy together, or you may just bless them with your bliss by chance in passing without even being aware of it. When we forget or reject our feminine home base we starve ourselves and our community of feminine radiance; creating an imbalance of energy, which fosters aggression, manipulation, perversion, depression, and confusion, isolation in our homes, communities, societies and our world.

I am not promoting a hedonistic, pleasure-centered life. Since the pleasure already lives within you, you don't need to make your life about the pursuit of pleasure. As women, pleasure is our birthright and our responsibility.

The first step toward becoming free in your expression of feminine energy is to let go of guilt surrounding your experiences of pleasure. Give the pleasure in you the space and opportunity to flow. It is one of your many gifts and you don't serve anyone by withholding it.

In the end, love is all. Self-love, loving others, being love, being in love, and acting in love – it is all the same. There is no sacrifice in love, we are not giving anything up or giving anything away, so there is no loss. We are expanding in love. We do not need to separate and divide ourselves from "others" to fuel our capacity for love. We do not need to separate our SELF in order to experience SELF-love.

How I Got My Wings Back:
A Story of Self Love
by Claudia Zebersky

"Respect yourself enough to walk away from anything that no longer serves you, grows you, or makes you happy."
– Robert Tew

Most of us marry with the best of intentions: to have kids, a happy, healthy home, being in a partnership, building a life together and when the kids are older, growing old and grey together. No one goes into a marriage *expecting* to get a divorce – but it happens. And it *happened to me.*

It took me a full year to accept that divorce would be part of my life experience before I finally made the decision. The fact that I would have to walk away from life as I knew it, in order to find a healthier and more balanced environment for me to thrive in, was very scary to me at the time. But I knew deep down in my core, I deserved better and most importantly, my children deserved to grow up in a loving environment. So I decided to give myself a second chance at love and life and to my surprise, divorce was one of the best decisions I've ever made. But it did not come easy and it pried me open to face my own childhood wounds that got me thinking: where did it all start and how did I end up here?

I remember one particular morning in middle school sitting in class with my other 45 classmates. I was twelve-years-old.

One of our teachers had a special exercise for all of us that day. We were instructed to move the 45 desks next to each other so we could form a circle and face one another. I was sitting next to my best friend and most trusted companion, Miriam. The teacher handed us a blank piece of paper and asked us to write our names on the top. I could feel the fear rising. *What does she wants us to do this for? Why is my name on the top of the page? What about my name? I do not want to be seen!*

As I was sitting there shaking, she then told us to pass the page to the person to the right of us, so we could write the first thing that came to mind about them. We only have a few seconds before another page was dropped in front of us. By then, my worst fear had become a reality. *What if someone says something bad about me? What do others think of me? I do not want to know!*

You see I was a shy introvert going through one of the most challenging times in my childhood. As I was approaching adolescence, parts of me were growing at different speeds and sizes. I was too skinny, my nose was too big, I hadn't figured out my hair, my chest never developed and I was one of the last girls to menstruate. I was very self-conscious of myself like many girls around that age. For me especially, coming from a very confident and high strung family, in particular my mother and my sister, who, by no coincidence, were two of the most sought-after and popular girls in their time. But that was totally not me. I felt like quite the opposite.

It was a constant reminder that I was not good enough and that there was something seriously wrong with me.

That was my biggest trigger and the button that when pushed, would unleash the biggest pain and trail of unworthiness in my life. And it all started that morning in my middle school classroom.

The exercise continued. I was panicking on the inside, looking to see who would get my paper. I was barely paying attention to the paper that touched my desk. I feared the worst. The teacher called out the end of the exercise and everyone proceeded to return the signed paper to its owner. The paper got dropped on my desk, and I feel like my heart is going to come out of me. I quickly scanned through some of the words on my page:

> Nice
> *Pana,* which means cool in Venezuelan
> Quiet
> And then…

There it was. It was the first word that jumped out of the page and went straight like a knife into my heart.

Fea, and yes, as you may guess, it means "ugly."

There it was, the 3-letter word that would set the tone for the next 17 years of my life.

It started my need to constantly seek validation from the outside and created my fears of being seen. I swore to myself, I would play it safe and would not expose myself in that way ever again, even though as a little girl, I had dreamed of being in a fairy tale relationship; the one where I would find the love of my life, unite with him and drift into a deep dance of love and sexuality (yes, from a very young age my soul was making those desires known.) But after that cold morning experience, I closed myself to that possibility, closed the connection to my own inner well-being and embarked on a journey to find meaning and love outside of myself.

I navigated different relationships; in some I was the pursuer; in others I waited for things to unfold. My first long-term relationship finally arrived when I was 20 years-old. And this time I was committed to making it work. I worked so hard to make it work that I must have blinded myself because I found myself being lied to and cheated on. I was heartbroken *again*.

From that point on, I made a conscious decision to not let love dictate my decisions, to close my heart and play it safe. Love seemed too scary and it seemed to make me vulnerable and set me up for pain. And so from that place, I chose the man who I would later marry. We built a life together, but we did not build a relationship. It seemed he wasn't ready to dive deeper into discovering himself either; he was in constant survival mode. We both played it safe and focused on the outside instead of the inside and very quickly our relationship became a struggle. We found ourselves miserable dealing with daily responsibilities and parenthood.

Shortly after delivering my second child, I knew something had to change. My children needed me fully present and functional and I could no longer sustain that while living a lie. So I made the biggest decision of my life: to leave my 7-year marriage to find myself on my own and create a life worth living.

I refused to allow myself to be disrespected and unhappy, and decided to create a life full of love and meaning, the life of my dreams, whatever it takes. And so I did.

All the pain, fear, and rejections in my life have taught me so much and have set me up to be the woman I am today and for that I am grateful. I've learned about my nature and the nature of the Universe and I feel supported and guided through every step of my journey of self-discovery.

It's now been two years since I made the biggest decision of my life and I am happy to report I feel stronger now than ever. I've overcome some of the biggest challenges of my life and I continue to walk through the path with faith and trust that I live in a loving Universe, continually showing me the way to my best self. I feel more beautiful than ever. My past no longer haunts me. I am grateful for every decision I made for it has taken me to where I am today.

I am a Goddess; a Warrior Goddess who's not afraid to walk through the fire time and time again.

For now, I know my mess makes my message. From my painful experiences, I have discovered my purpose. I came to earth with a message of love and transformation. I came at this time to remind you about the power of love, the power of choosing a better life for yourself. You are powerful, you are worthy, and you are all you need to create a life worth living. I am here to remind you no matter how bad your current circumstances may seem, you are one decision away from your best life. The Universe is waiting for your command and it responds to your willingness to change; you do not need to know all the answers, only that you want answers and change, and it will send them your way.

There's magic waiting to be discovered deep inside you. Allow yourself to feel the pain and the joy and choose to love yourself despite life's setbacks. The Universe adores you and wants the best for you, so be prepared to be delighted.

I am no longer afraid to be seen or afraid of what others think of me. I circle back to that morning exercise and tell that small girl, "Do not worry. You are more beautiful than you ever imagined. You are loved and you will touch many people's lives. Trust yourself."

This is just the beginning for me as I am preparing myself to come out and spread my wings wide open. I want to continue to be an example for other women who have felt trapped and scared and to inspire them to step into their brilliance and beauty.

Every day I fall more deeply in love with myself more as I graciously claim my place in the world.

Now it's your turn.

Are you ready to open yourself up to life and second chances? Say YES to yourself and spread your wings wide open and get ready to receive the life of your wildest dreams.

"She was finally *ready* to show her *true self* to the *world* and so she *spread* her *wings*"

© Aera Productions

Letting Go of My Locks
by Jemine Omabegho

Last week I cut off my locks, the single longest hairstyle I have ever had.

I had been thinking of cutting them off because they seemed to be breaking and popping off every few days. My brother would say, "Well, that's where you were stressed and your body is just getting rid of all the things that have caused you the most stress": being blindsided by a breakup and moving from Philadelphia to Chicago; being unemployed for 10 months and then finally landing my dream job; and, a roommate who refused to pay the bills and her rent.

"No, _we_ aren't moving; _I_ am moving and I don't want to be with you anymore."

Those were the fateful words I heard almost two years ago from the man I considered the love of my life. This came after he had me look over his job offer letter to see if there were any aspects of the offer that should be renegotiated.

It was the second time in my life words took the breath out of me and forced me to find a seat. Now I get why people always ask, "Are you sitting down?" before breaking you the bad news. After my mother's death, this breakup was the most heartbreaking experience of my first 30 years. You must understand; I loved Derrick with all of my being and had put off a move to Chicago or DC at the behest of our families, who like me, thought Derrick and I were moving on to marriage or creating a family. His father and stepmom would often introduce me as their "future daughter-in-law."

© Joni Jones

When his dad said those words I felt a part of a family, especially since my mother's passing in 2001 it had been difficult to feel bonded with my family. Since we all handled the grief differently, I felt we pushed each other away. My father basically left my brother and I to start a new life on his own. My brother was living in Ohio and enjoying it for the most part, so in the meantime Derrick's family and I forged our own relationships with each other; his sisters, mom and step-mom often communicated with me more than they did with Derrick.

One time, his father and step-mom invited my girlfriends and I to go to a wine festival without Derrick. As he was drinking his coffee that day he says, "I feel as though I am no longer needed." Since we had talked about moving our relationship into the marriage stage eventually, I thought it was important for me to have these strong relationships in place and help create our new family.

I was wrong about my family not being there though. When it seemed like my soul was breaking during the next few months: sleepless nights, intense drinking, internal bleeding leading to hospital visits, extreme weight loss, crying into Ben and Jerry's and the loss of my independent fun and free spirit, my father and brother would call me daily to offer me words of support and love or just to check in to see how I was managing. My father would say, "Well at least you aren't married with kids!" True I suppose.

After the break up, I stalked his page relentlessly, trying to see what he was doing, how he was doing, or if he missed me? We would talk on the phone, and he was encouraging about my move to Chicago if it was for me and not for us. Much to many people's chagrin, I still made the move to Chicago in hopes of reconciling but also since I've wanted to be here for years. *I had wanted to move to the city after my mother told me during a visit there that she saw me living in the city.* After he insisted I came on a certain day in order for him to help me move in, I made my journey to Chicago. Fifteen hours, two terrified cats, and zero bathroom breaks later, I finally made it to the Windy City. I was ready for my new adventure, a rebirth, and perhaps my love realizing we were meant to be together.

Cocktail Recipe
EX-BF Go Fuck Yourself

Ingredients:
- 2 shots of tequila
- Teaspoon fresh squeezed lime juice
- Club soda
- Ice
- Anger, tears and realization we need to move the fuck on
  are the special ingredients
- Stir or shake all those things together. Best enjoyed while
  watching the Real Housewives of some city and accompanied
  by a pint of Ben and Jerry's

But I had barely arrived when he hit me with some news. As I was taking up the back of the U-Haul to unload the boxes and see the apartment he had found for me, he was texting furiously to someone. I ask him what he was doing and he then told me he was dating someone new. One month after he moved to Chicago, barely two months after our breakup. The feeling of the knife in my heart went even deeper. *Are you fucking serious? Already? You are already in a fucking relationship? What the fuck?* was all I could keep saying. Mentally I had to have a new mantra – *Well I am going to show you how happy I can be without you.* But painfully I would say to him, *You must not have loved me at all if you could move on so quickly. Did you meet this woman on your interview out here? How could you go back on this?* He would say, "It's just fun. We are talking, nothing serious. Well, we'll hang out again once it reaches 70 degrees." I looked forward to the first 70 degree day, though that was months away from Oct 2013. I would message him to see how he was doing and it would turn into me crying and longing for the man I used to know, not the one who nonchalantly shattered my heart into a million pieces.

LOVING IN THE CITY

Many people have asked me how was I able to establish myself in a new city where the only people I knew were Derrick and my friend Heather. Well it wasn't easy that is for sure, especially with heartbreak looming over my soul and energy. Initially I started going up to random people in bars and making conversation. I met some of my closest friends on public transportation or out and about in the city. I thought, *wow people in this city are nice, willing to help you out and are the most attractive I've seen in a while.* Within my first few weeks I was invited to parties, art shows and a Chanukah celebration. Was this how becoming part of a community starts? Yes.

On my adventures in the city, I took lots of photos just to separate myself from the photos of him and me on Facebook. Soon I found taking these photos of my "new life" in Chicago, really meant starting to actually enjoy myself. Laughter came back to me, smiles came easier and adventures were something I would jump to. The people here are wonderful, the music scene is great and the culmination of all of that seemed to make the breakup transition a bit easier.

A few months after moving to Chicago, I decided to go out on some dates, fun ones to just get back into the saddle and a few serious ones. Sometimes I would feel guilt come over me, even though I was clearly not doing anything wrong since Derrick had moved on. It was then I finally understood my happiness is dictated by <u>me</u>. Not being in relationship with Derrick doesn't make me hopeless and tragically single; it makes me independent, strong and happy. Dating in my 30s is a bit amusing actually. I've been out on dates with a delivery driver – he asked me out for Indian food and then when the check came told me he couldn't pay for either one of us (I even caught him stealing change out of my purse); an actor – charismatic and a ladies man; a CEO – for our first date he took me to two of the most expensive restaurants in the city (that was entirely too much; it overwhelmed me) and then proceeded to tell me all the salacious things he wanted to do to me in his hotel room – of course I declined the offer; numerous online dates where they say they are 5'6" and in reality are 5'2". Ugh! I have seen it all, but love and relish in the freedom to do what I want, when I want to without having to answer to anyone. On the other hand, it would be nice to be able to share my life with someone.

Derrick truly was the love of my life to date, and for all of the years and moments we had together I will cherish always. It is rare to love someone completely, and having had that experience I am forever grateful and would not trade it for anything. Our relationship was built on mutual respect; we supported each other's dreams, picked each other up when the other would fall, and made fun of each other's quirkiness. He would help me with my schoolwork and encourage and motivate me to continue nurturing my art. Of course it was not all peaches and cream if one could just leave someone all willy-nilly, get a new girlfriend and stay with her for nearly as long as we were in a relationship. Clearly we lacked the ability to communicate or else I wouldn't have felt blindsided.

LETTING GO OF MY LOCKS

As I looked at all of my locks on the floor the weight of some of the anger came up. The stresses that were causing my hair to fall out were being realized. *How could a man I gave myself to so completely and unguardedly just dismiss me like that? How could he move on to an uglier version of me? How could he say he wanted to be with someone who was a professional who didn't need to be taken care of and then be with someone who is exactly the opposite? How can my friends describe her as "such a lovely sweet girl, but always dates men who can take care of her?"* Ok. So the guy who doesn't want to take care of anyone and just wants to worry about himself is doing the exact opposite of everything he is telling me. *How could he be so flippant with my emotions? What the actual fuck? What level of perfection was he looking for?* When we were living together, he would get massaged daily, since he would complain about aches from working out; I came home and cooked for us about four days a week; I went to his friends' parties even though he would rarely come to my friends' parties. Every birthday he had I would take off and create a spa day for him and make him all his favorite meals. One day I even had a surprise party for him, managed to get all his friends together, even ones I had never met, and his family to come into town. While he had a great night that night, the first response wasn't thank you but I hate surprise parties; don't ever do this again. *How could I satisfy him and make him happy and he never noticed?*

These were the stresses my tresses were feeling. Somewhere I lost my own voice and my hair was trying to motivate me to be happy and content. This is why my locks wanted to free themselves from my head. The beauty about cutting off my hair was that it freed me of the anger and resentment and has allowed me to appreciate love for what it is: something imperfect, difficult at times, but worth fighting for.

I am part of a community now, where they push me to be

better; encourage my cooking and art, are there when I need a shoulder to cry on or a drinking buddy. My life is going well. Single but okay with it. I have a great job in the city utilizing my Bachelor's degree, great friends and the best relationship with my dad and brother. They truly have been my keystone throughout this whole journey. Sure, I still think of Derrick fondly– get out of my damn head already – but this new journey is about me and my happiness and not his. Now is the time for me to take a page out of his book, and think about what I can get out of this situation. Who knows what the future will hold? *Will I stay in financial technology? Will I become the black version of Ina Garten and Martha Stewart? Will I find love? Will I buy my own home?* So many questions and uncertainty, but what I do know is that in the meantime I just need to enjoy this ride that is life.

Learning How To Swim

by Ta-Shana Taylor

"Just keep swimming, just keep swimming, just keep swimming, swimming, swimming."
~Finding Nemo

But Dory, what if I don't know how to swim?

Finding Nemo is one of my favorite movies, and Dory is one of my favorite characters. However, every time I heard this ditty it made me hate her a little. There was also something about a message telling me to keep swimming that made me resentful. When I first watched the movie, I was in my second year of graduate school and I was swimming as hard and as fast as I could to keep my head above the turbulent waters of my life. It was as if Dory was accusing me of not working hard enough. And I honestly wanted to stop swimming; it was wearing me down and I was losing myself in it all. To hear Dory cheerfully tell me that everything would be alright if I just kept doing what I was already doing, made me want to get a harpoon and put her on my dinner plate. Instead, I drowned in my own burnout.

It wasn't until ten years later that I finally decided to learn how to swim. I'd had enough of sitting on the shore watching everyone else live a life that seemed limitless and so easy. I wanted to enjoy the water, instead of only surviving it.

I had moved to Miami, and the sparkling azure oceans called to me. Growing up in Queens, New York, I had never learned how to swim. But now I was ready for a different lifestyle, one where I felt I could do anything, one where I could fully enjoy the beauty of the entire world. I had worked hard and was ready to reap my rewards by having a relaxed life in southern Florida.

One summer I found the perfect swim school where I could get one-on-one instruction. I approached learning how to swim with the same mentality I approached everything in my life: with the brutal force of my determined will. Nothing was going to stop me; I was going to beat this. I was going to obliterate my lack of skill. I was going to grow and move forward in my life by any means necessary.

At first I excelled, like I often do. I was a champ at doing bobs, my form in kicking was a dream, my float was perfect, and my breathing was impeccably timed. I came to class early and stayed late. All the instructors said they'd never seen a more dedicated student. Then when it came time to actually swim, I struggled. My technique was fine and I was strong enough. But no matter what I did, my body dragged in the water. Somehow I was sinking like a lead weight.

"You're supposed to glide on the surface of the water. I don't know why you keep sinking," my swim instructor remarked with frustration. I didn't know either. She demonstrated the freestyle to me once again, for what felt like the gazillionth time. It looked so effortless when she did it. I could hear Dory taunting me, whispering *"Just keep swimming, just keep swimming..."*

The familiar frustration was back. I've been here a thousand times before. Constantly working hard, just so that I can stay exactly where I am. Always moving, but never actually progressing.

No matter how hard I work, I'm barely making it. I'm an educated woman with a great job that pays me just enough to get by, but not enough to build a life. I work two jobs in the hopes that one day maybe I'll own a home, but I've been doing this for almost ten years and I still rent. I go out socializing and have a healthy network of people I know. But it's been months since I've been on a date and only a few people I consider true friends. My family lives a quick drive away, but I rarely see them. I eat fairly healthy, but my thirty-something body keeps packing on the weight.

To me it seemed as if everything was a reminder that I would never have the life that I dreamed of. And swimming was becoming one of the many things on my list that proved I wasn't good enough. No matter what I did, no matter how hard I tried, I'd never be good enough.

I considered quitting. *Why bother? Nothing will ever change. This is my life and I should just get used to it.* But then I heard Dory saying, *"Just keep swimming, swimming, swimming."* The irony of her words finally sunk in. If there were ever a situation in life that called for more swimming, this would be it. After all, that's what you do when you're first learning how to do anything, right?

Learning how to swim wasn't an option for me; I couldn't survive yet another failure. But I knew I needed to do things differently. No longer could I just put in lots of hours in the hopes that if I did it long enough, everything would work out. This time I decided to reach out and ask for help. Even though my friends knew I was finally learning to swim, I felt stupid asking for help. My brain kept chastising me: *you should know how to do this already. You're 35 years old and you can't even manage to do something little children know how to do.* But as I reached out, I came into contact with a tsunami of support. The swell of advice, good luck, and friends cheering me along carried me high in the water. The waves of love and gratitude were washing me quickly along.

It had never occurred to me that I was surrounded by people who knew how to swim and wanted to see me swim alongside them. I wasn't alone in this. I had more friends than I realized. My community was showing me I could trust them, and if I could trust them maybe I could trust the water. And maybe, just maybe, I could also trust myself.

Dory was whispering in my ear, *"Yes, trust. It's what friends do."*

From this support, I received some very specific swimming techniques and strategies I could try. But mostly, everyone gave me only one piece of advice:

Relax.

The problem was, I didn't even know what that word meant. I knew how to sit around and do nothing for short periods of time, but I didn't know how to relax. I'd heard of the word, but the actual concept was foreign to me.

Buoyed by the newfound trust in myself and others, I decided it was time to learn how to relax and trust God. I hadn't realized that I never trusted Him until that summer. I didn't even realize that my relationship with Him would have anything to do with swimming. But every time I sank in the water, I could feel Him look down on me in disappointment. And I felt resentful that He never helped me. How can I relax when I didn't feel that God was on my side?

But swimming is an act of trust. Trusting that the water—the very thing that looks like nothing, the very thing that could kill you—could actually support you and carry you. Maybe that's why water is so sacred in all religions?

The next time I arrived to class early, I did nothing but

breathe and float until class started. Lying on my back, arms spread out with the sun in my face, the sound of water in my ears, and my heart open to the world, I realized I had everything I needed to learn how to swim. When my instructor arrived, at the start of the lesson she ran me through the normal drills to warm up. But this time the drills weren't helpful, they were distracting. I had made space in my life for God and my swim instructor's rigidness was messing with my flow. It dawned on me that rigid structure was just a way to compensate for lack of trust.

I had outgrown what had always worked for me. Luckily, when the student is ready, the teacher will appear.

The very next lesson, my normal swim instructor had some family matters to attend to and I got a substitute instructor for a week. He didn't do drills or structure. Instead he assessed my skill level, and quickly determined that my problem was that I was taking it all too seriously and wasn't enjoying any of it. He also picked up that I was competitive and figured he could use that to get me to loosen up and have fun.

"Want to play a game?" he asked. Of course I did. I love games! More accurately, I love winning. And games let me do that. He grabbed three bright colored rubber rings. And threw each of them into the pool. "Go get 'em."

I jumped in, and swam out away from the edge of the pool with excitement, hoping to catch some of them before they floated to the bottom. Diving down I would grab one, swim to the second, dive down again and retrieved that one, and this continued. When I finally had them all in my hand, I came up to the surface bearing my prizes triumphantly.

"Again!" I exclaimed, like a kid demanding another ride on

the rollercoaster. I hadn't even noticed how effortless my swimming had become. I had lost myself in the sheer joy of the experience.

"Okay, but this time we're going to make it harder." He threw one ring into the water and said "Freestyle out to the ring, grab it, tread for ten counts, float on your back for five counts, and then backstroke back to the ledge." I was off. We did this for two hours. I didn't even realize I was swimming the entire time. We didn't waste time discussing technique or form. He didn't stop me from swimming so he could demonstrate the right way to do something. We just played. I was like a puppy playing fetch and having a blast at it. Finally, I was weightlessly gliding on the surface of that pool. I always knew I was strong enough, but now I also knew the water had my back and that I didn't need to work to stay afloat. God was with me and He is always trying to support me, if I just let Him.

I went home starving, exhausted, and exhilarated in a way I couldn't remember feeling in a long time. I was actually having fun while accomplishing something. It was deeply satisfying.

From that day, my swimming quickly progressed. And more importantly, I didn't have to work hard to make it happen. Now I'm able to move forward in my life in a way that doesn't burn me out, but instead allows me to form deeper connections to myself, my community, and God. Maybe that's what He wants for us all?

"Just keep swimming, just keep swimming, just keep swimming, swimming, swimming."

I finally understand what Dory had been trying to say to me for over a decade. It's the same reason why she was always my favorite character. Dory was telling me to let go and trust that everything will be okay.

That's the key to learning how to swim.

HEALING

The Toolbox

by Milina Franke

I Am Thankful
For all the attention and unblocked flow
We share, give, and receive at all times.
This is not what it feels like to be far away.
All thoughts and/or perceived "Problems"
Are but constructs of my own mind.
There... there is that ringing in my left ear
I wish...I choose... to detox and purify to the point of not
manifesting physical symptoms...

Simply put:
I Am a Clear Channel
Which expresses Freely,
Physically, Emotionally, Energetically, Mentally.

At this time, we feel very
Susceptible to exterior suggestion
Thus, we ground and shield.
I... I feel Super obvious with my
Ever fluctuating state of being.

Running Lines of Musical Madness
Courses through the air.
It quickens pace, chasing about a heartbeat.

Sincerely,
We Who Witness

© Jaamal Clark

YOU STAY, WE STAY

You leave, we leave.
Either way, it makes a difference to
Me.

These
Are the decisions we make
To step our game up.
To stand steadfast and strong.

Because,
Ummm
This is what *Life* is:
The decision to stand our ground.
We choose to keep going
We choose to keep moving
We choose to keep growing
and glowing
Along...

The Way.

Choosing the best inside
Of me.

We choose to remain unattached and happy.
We choose to keep hope alive
And Well.

Aspire and dream for more.
We hold our voice
Strong and steady.
Strong and steady.
Steady and strong.

As Saul Williams says,
"Outta Darkness,
    Comes
      A 'Boom.
        Boom.
          BOOM...'"

_~_~_~_~_~_

THE GODDESS ROOM

Safe, sacred space, cloaked in red.
    Ahhhhh...

How fitting to appreciate an often utilized color of youth.
Lying here, she states out loud,

    "I am open."
    "Communicate."
    "Masters, Teachers, Students, Elementals,
    God/Goddess,
        Guides..."
    "Experience crystal clear communication within."
    "Assimilate and see."

Hands on heart,
Warmth emanating upon breast,
She falls.

One found one of another sex.
Dapperly dressed
Suit and tie.

Member of the underbelly,
    Yes!
Considered,

More or less
Considered a "spy"
Light being from another Side.

Drawing in one
     Deep...........Breath
Watching this other "she"
Walk through a door
Slowly.

CRACK!

We feel warmth in/of chest.

She falls...
Spirit is pulled
Up to body.
While experiencing the love embrace.

Death
She hears a voice,
The heart
Whispering

    "Here,
    We Shall Start."

-~-~-~-~-~-

WE ARE, I AM, MY OWN GREATEST LESSON.

Sometimes, we stumble,
Much as a doe's wobbling first steps.
Images paint a skeleton picture
Until and always in person
The scene...

Eye witness.
  I Manifest.

-~-~-~-~-~-

SPIRIT TAKES CARE OF EVERYTHING

The day unveils itself, flowing steadily.
With mystery.

Moments make me wonder out loud.
Out loud.
Out loud.

A sleeping babe slumbers no more.
Complete that which you begin.
All else moves easily into swing.
Where are you going? Who will you Be?
Upon bended knee... We see.
Flee the scene, which "You" always thought "you knew."
Something new to do.

Strike that.
  Reverse It.
    Surrender.

Listen to the voices in your heart-head.
The soft, reassuring ones.
Wise ones
Free of any dread.

This is for you.
  Feel It.

We Always Knew.
        Truth.

Through and through.
Sun. Moon.
Above. Below.
Code Bleu.

-~-~-~-~-~-

LETTER OF THANK YOU

Dear Sister,

As I sit here, preparing to send over my draft, the deep urge to just... Thank You... wells up. Since our first meeting, I have been left in a state of sheer excited awe. You inspire me to strive more, enjoy the simple things, and always...

Remain True to My Voice.

The level of unconditional love has been overwhelmingly, exquisitely beautiful. There are days where the tears flow, out of sadness, outta happiness, and every single little breath-taking nuance in between.

Dear Sister, you show and remind me to...
               See,
               Feel,
               And Cherish the
               Light and Medicine
               in Life, Nature,
               Everyone.
               Primarily the

Viscous Pisces,
Myself.

Thank You.

Throughout exploration, such swings of melancholy and
sheer bliss arise.
The self-induced exploitative experiential fluctuations of
this chosen incarnate – "Me" – flow forth, gracious and
unbridled.

And awkward.
Oh, the "social anxiety."
Bewildering, really.
Pfftt.
I digress.

Such quandaries arise:

"What is authenticity?"
"What is transparency?"
"What is genuine?"
"How clearly can I reflect the blessing of life?"
"How can I be of service"
"Who am I?"
...Well, you know, the gambit of floating thought-clouds
translated and tingling throughout the course of an
energetic-physical Being aligning with a Soul Porpoise.
(Pun ... er... Intended)

The REALLY Fun Stuff.

I find myself just... wishing... to learn and pay all due
respect with fellow brother and sisters, all the while
honoring our ancestors within a flawless blending of the
ancient and present.

Joyfully. Progressively.

... I have a LOT of work to do.

I am organized. I ALWAYS Follow Through.

So be it.

The very fine line tippy top apex of this, my dear Inspirational Motivator, has coalesced into the reflection and writing of something bigger than me...

Simply,... this breath and agreed upon joyful, tangible "thing," project, passing of musings..."

This. which has been penned by hand, to share and over/under/inner Stand.

"She Loved Herself."

While withdrawing, yearning so very, very nothing and much at all to be the Highest, most Clear and Pure Version of Me...

I admire from afar the glory of these goddesses processing and sharing with unwavering authenticity for this belief-unveiling book.

I subsequently and always believe in each and every one of these women so, so much.

In our vision.
     In our mission.
          In our being.
               In our love.

In our light.

Our internal states reflect.
Concentric Circles.

Daydreams dance within our reality.
Bless.

I have towed the line for days on end, feeling into, day-
dreaming, envisioning, manifesting, actualizing, night-
owling into how "best" to highlight the mysterious and
expansive Human Spirit.

I wonder if I am doing right<>left by my "fellow man." I
stumble about, grasping onto wisps of clarity for brief
moments, reveling in their expanses and yearning to
BE THE CHANGE, "Walk the Walk," or <at the very least>
pretend to "Fake it until I make it" until putting these silly
games aside to just smile and be happy.
Because we are always here. Encouraging and exploring
hand in hand, all the while cheering along our seen and
unseen friends. Baby steps. Infinity. Beyond.

Thank you for pulling down inspiration and organizing it so
that We can be Our Highest Serving Expression of Self and
Bounce our Evolution Expression of Our Soul Nature's
Best.

It feels soft, as if I know nothing and all rolled into one. I
have written drafts and bullet points and sketched and
gazed upon the wind in trees under setting suns. I stay
inside for days, and stare at walls long enough until the fire
burns, engulfing all into ***ACTION!*** once more.

We have been here many times before. Always, Always,
Always, there is a new promising door.

After playing with premises, titles, and varying such process, I have decide to follow the excitement and spirit. With humility, I submit various scribbles on paper, from "My Diary."

Sometimes, We are more connected than we could ever possibly conceive. I am young. I am old. I am someone. I am no one. I am anything Eye can Conceive.

And so are you.
And so are we.

{You... Are... AMAZING! }

May All Beings Everywhere Be Happy and Free.
I Love You.
Thank You.
Bula.

Milina

-~-~-~-~-~-

Beauty Is Formless.
Shifting Manifestations
Revealing it's Self
To Us;
Open.
Appreciate.
See.

-~-~-~-~-~-

All I Know,
I Am Amazed By The Fact.
We All Share the Same Story...

Insecurity.

It Is Astonishing.
A Shift.
Relinquish This.
The Fear, Pessimism, Doubt...
I Drop All Of It.
No Use Holding On.
It is Time to Practice
A New Song.
Dream and Share
With
Loving Care.
Watch Sparkles in the Sun
Before,
Temporarily,
I Disappear.

P.E.A.C.E.

1

Kindly Return all Tools to Box.
Keep Your Skill Set Honed
        Clean and Ready.
"There Will Be A Brighter Day."

Perfectly Imperfect:
Learning to Love My Crazy

by Stephanie Loewenstern

"I love your crazy," a woman who I highly admire once said to me.

I chose to hear, *"You're fucking crazy and you're right, everyone hates you."* A STORY I have been telling myself for two and a half decades.

If I had a penny for every time someone said I was crazy, weird, "too much," or insane; I would be flying jets, sleeping on yachts, or taking that trip to Bali and living on an Island like I have always dreamed of.

If I had a nickel for every time I blamed my circumstances for my choices, I would be paying off the Master's degree I never completed, have the liposuction and breast lift that I have always wanted, and live in the mansion in Malibu with an ocean side view – far enough away from the people in my home town.

Imagine a life shifting away from the present moment, and stepping into the space of "poor me, why me, or woe is me."

How about these voices inside my head? The one that says there is:

"Never enough money, bags, clothes, food and never enough good men.

I am never going to be rich, thin, pretty, sexy, and wanted."

Then I hear the voice louder:

"I wish I never said that.

Are they talking about me? Should I have done that?

Yes! I am awesome. No, you fucking suck.

Ugh why did I wear this out?

Did I gain weight again?

At least my boobs look okay.

Shit, there is a stain on my shirt.

Fuck, my car is a mess.

I should have gone to the party.

I should change jobs because my boss hates me.

I could have done that better.

Did I drink too much again last night?

Ugh he hates me. She hates me.

I am annoying.

He is going to leave me anyway."

When did my worthiness conversations start to define my choices?

When did I choose to decide I was no longer a graceful, worthy, innocent soul?

Was it when Mark stole my first kiss?

When whisky first burned my throat with desire?

Maybe it was the time Scott robbed my innocence during a blackout on the eve of my 17th birthday?

Hmmm maybe when the love of my life, Mike, stood me up on the night of my senior homecoming, leaving me pained by the righteousness of my worthiness conversations.

Or that time I met white snow, in Panama City on college spring break with another fraternity brother.

Guilt and shame had me when I almost died in a car accident walking away without a bruise, consequence, or scar from the scene.

It could be the passing of my two great soul sisters Esther and Amber. Maybe that's the reason. They are gone, you are alive, which makes you one fucked up human being after all the shit you have done.

"The world is out to get me."

Self-loathing, self-pain, and self- hatred; three humiliating truths I've found comfort in too well. *"I am fucked up. I will never change. He is right about me."*

Yoga. Alcoholics Anonymous. Switching jobs. Transformational trainings. Gaining weight. Losing weight. Drinking again. Not drinking again. Therapy. Starting grad school. Leaving grad school. Dating men. Not dating men. Juice cleanses. Half marathons. Temple. Switching friends. Moving to big cities.

■■

Stillness, surrender, trust, and forgiveness and then I finally began to let go of the conversation that I was fucked up or crazy.

"I'm sorry," stopped rolling off the tip of my tongue like I was a fucking apology.

Wherever I go, I always am. I finally chose to surrender.

I surrendered to myself.

The ugly, messy and perfectly imperfect self.

The self that loves, that gives, that receives, and experiences joy.

The self that connects with her vulnerability, her creativity, and her passion.

The self that is creative, fun, and sometimes afraid.

The self who forgives herself when she falls and lifts herself back up with grace.

The self that cries, that laughs, dances, plays, and explores her sensual side, her feminine divine self, and her sacred self.

The self that knows its okay to be in the dark and that the light will always shine brighter.

That this too shall pass, and that in her darkest moments she finds her strength.

I surrendered to the innocent, perfect, holy self that she is.

The inspirational, confident, compassionate, loving divinity.

I choose to surrender to myself; to simply exist in my power and accept the perfectly imperfect woman that I AM.

Forgiveness, surrender, trust, and self-love are a practice. Becoming present to the voice inside precipitates the gates to freedom.

When I CHOSE to be the love and light in this world my life transformed. My stories and circumstances of my past no longer kept me in the dark.

I am beautiful. I am loving. I am enough. I am worthy. I love you Stephanie. I fucking love you. You are a rock star.

The new voices in my head; through the practice of recognizing the voices that used to run the show.

The darkness of my cocoon is a comfort I knew so well.

Breaking down the walls of the cocoon is a messy evolution.

Breakdown after breakdown, followed by the powerful breakthrough over and over again. The journey never stops, as I never know everything.

I have the choice, to surrender to the love and divinity within myself.

And so I choose to surrender into the free butterfly that I already am.

Nothing beautiful is ever perfect. And so it is, I am perfectly imperfect, and that is okay by me ☺

How I Learned to Love My Yoni

by Suki Eleuterio

It wasn't a part of me for the longest time. I pretended it didn't exist.

Well, you see it was just easier that way. To avoid it, not touch it, not look at it, and certainly never talk about it. That's not what a good girl does.

The first time I felt shame about it was when I noticed I had a hair. Yes, a hair...down there. It was the first time I realized I was no longer a little girl; I was becoming a woman. But I hated that. I didn't want to be a grown up. Grown ups didn't seem to have fun. They always seemed stressed out and angry. Was this going to be my life now?

I tried to make the hair stop but it kept coming. Every time it grew I felt my childhood slipping away. None of the other girls had hair, I knew from the locker rooms. They were all still little girls and here I was growing up too fast, unable to turn back the hands of time.

It wasn't surprising to me that I was the first girl in class to get her period. I was twelve years old. It came slowly and painfully.

The day my period came I was at my cousins' house. My aunt made me take a cold bath. She gave me a monster-sized pad and a cup of tea saying, "You are a woman now, you know Suki. You should be proud. You're the first of your cousins to become a woman."

My cousins were all beaming at me excitedly asking me what it felt like to be a woman and I wanted to curl up in a ball and lock myself in my room. I was miserable. This part of me – this place with hair that sometimes felt nice and sometimes felt painful, this place that my family told me never to touch or talk about, this mysterious, interesting, strange, exotic place was now...bleeding.

As if there could be anything more that could disconnect me from it. I hated it. I wished it away.

I imagined myself still as a little girl, climbing trees and being a tomboy. In that moment I forgot I was bleeding, cramping, and emotional. And I lifted away.

This became an ongoing pattern for me; a disassociation with my body. When my period came, the pain was so intense I would feel like vomiting or blacking out. At first I thought this was normal; this was just going to be part of my life. But as more girls in my class started getting their periods too, I realized something was wrong. These other girls didn't have to stop everything when it was their time of the month. They didn't have seven full days of intense pain and exhaustion. They went about their lives while my body just went into shut down mode.

This suffering continued all through high school and college. The more pain I felt, the more I shut down any connection I had to this mysterious place. But every now and then I would be strangely drawn to it – like a moth to a flame. Why did it cause me pleasure and then cause me pain? What did it all mean?

The word "yoni" is a Sanskrit term meaning vagina, womb,

sacred space or source of all life. It was originally associated with the Goddess Shakti or Devi, the divine mother and it is one of the most beautiful words I have come across for this female body part that lies between my legs.

For years I would feel uncomfortable even saying "down there" let alone calling it "vagina" or "pussy." I hated those words; they felt so dirty and shameful. My Muslim and Christian background added additional layers of shame to my already fledgling perception of my body. Words like "sin" and "vulgar" and "filthy" would come to mind when I thought about sex or masturbation. There was nothing pure about it – there was nothing spiritual or divine about it. The vagina was just a horrible place that was best ignored, rejected, or silenced.

And so I fell into a silence. I allowed the pain and shame and disgust and disassociation to take over. These periods of silence were only disrupted by unhealthy sexual choices and wild escapades, only followed by more periods of shame and silence. It was a toxic cycle. I had started to truly hate my vagina, I had started to say things like "my useless uterus."

In 2011 when I found out I had endometriosis, a painful disease that causes adhesions to form outside the uterus lining, I wasn't even that surprised. No wonder I had been in so much pain all my life. No wonder my period was so much worse than the other girls in school. It all made so much sense. Unfortunately for me, finding out this diagnosis and the subsequent surgery I had to endure only made me disconnect even more.

When we experience constant pain, it's easier to float away and pretend it doesn't exist. It's easier to blame the body part. "My malfunctioning uterus," I used to say. Or "my useless uterus." While recovering from surgery I thought about all the ways I hated my yoni. I hated it for making me grow up too soon. I hated it for putting me through years of pain. I hated it for giving me some strange disease. I hated it for making me go through invasive surgery. The scars were a reminder of my discontent. The bleeding was a reminder of my internal wounds and the unrest I was carrying with me.

The year after my surgery I gained weight, I broke out in acne, and I struggled with a new kind of depression. I call it my walking depression because although I was walking about, experiencing my life, hanging out with friends and going to social events, inside I was crumbling and falling apart. I was at my weakest. My world revolved around these wounds from my surgery. No amount of outside stimulation or downing alcoholic drinks was making me feel better.

One day I just cried – no, I sobbed – in the shower. I watched as the blood glided down the drain and I wondered if I was ever going to be normal again.

You can feel normal again.

It took me years but I slowly began to heal. My body started healing first. Slowly but surely the internal wounds felt a little less raw. The body is miraculous because it knows how to heal itself. The scars formed, the bleeding slowed, and I began to feel a little more "normal."

But when you heal, you must also heal your mind and your spirit. I began to recognize that although my wounds had healed, my battle was still on going. I was still fighting with this shame and guilt and disconnection.

My period came infrequently, just as it had all through my

teenage years. When it came, I was knocked off my feet in pain. What was going on? I thought the surgery would take this all away?

The divine has a way of teaching you through pain. Leading you through the mud to get to the sunlight. There's no easy way through.

I'm grateful for the wounds and the pain for they have made me who I am today.

I discovered Chi (or energy) from a Traditional Chinese doctor who gave me a herb supplement that made my period come like clockwork every month. She helped me discover that I had an energy block in my sacral chakra. As soon as I found this out, I wanted to know everything about the chakra and energy healing.

Through yoga and Reiki, I started to get in touch with a part of myself that I had ignored for so many years.

No, to be honest, a part of myself I hated.

I wanted to be that good little girl so much that I had allowed the abuse, allowed the detachment, allowed the defilement, allowed the cutting into, the rawness, the pain, the pure masochism of forgetting my yoni.

What was my yoni?

My God. I didn't even know.

No wonder the energy was blocked. I turned the tap off. I wouldn't even allow my period out. I had held on for so long, I didn't know what it meant to flow, to release, to let go.

Is that what it feels like? Like that first cry when you haven't cried for years? Those salty tears and the lump that rises in your throat. And the way your heart feels open after you cry?

When my period returned and the energy started moving again, I noticed inside me a shift into my higher self. A connection with my spirit that I had never felt before.

Flowing.

Like the river.

Goddess. Imperfect. Indestructible. Divine. Filled with unlimited love.

I was looking at it, feeling it, experiencing it. I was one with it.

It was a part of me. My yoni. It was like my hair or my eyes or my smile.

It was divine. Created by the creator. Unique and warm and loving.

Why was I so scared of it?

And the minute I embraced it. Truly loved it. Told myself for the first time,

"I
Love
You
Yoni."

Then a miracle happened. I was blessed with something I never thought I'd experience.

God gave me a child. God placed a little tiny soul inside my uterus...the same uterus I thought was useless. The same place I had hated for so long, now was a place filled with love.

The love between my husband and I had created this amazing new soul inside me. And my yoni...MY YONI was carrying this child.

My cervix, once cut open and raw, was now the gate keeper protecting this baby. It was now carrying and working and nurturing.

This was love. This was self love. This is what it finally meant to love myself. To love my yoni.

I never thought I'd see that day.

But as I sit here today, I am so overcome with gratitude. For all of me. Every part. For the pain, for the disconnection, for the days I didn't know who I was. Because I needed that darkness to find my light. And now that I'm here, I never want to go back.

As we step into the light, as a family, I will know that my yoni is mine.

And it is beautiful, and it is scarred, and it is perfect and imperfect, and tragic, and beautiful.

But it is mine.

The Way to Self-Love:
A Reflection on Comparison and Love

by Allison Dienstman

How do I stop comparing myself to others? Reminders of the things I don't have constantly parade in front of me. I feel insecure looking at pictures of others who seem happier, prettier, or more successful than me. I go on Facebook to see others reaching all the programmed milestones like getting married, having kids, or buying a house. Attractive and wealthy people flood my television screen each time I turn it on. Standing in line at the grocery store, images of "perfect" women stare back at me with their airbrushed faces and obsessively fit bodies.

I look around and compare, compare, compare, measuring myself to the standards of others.

Of course, in doing so I'll only face disappointment because I know that I'll never be the prettiest, richest, smartest, most loved, or most popular person. Sometimes I feel so overwhelmed with what I don't have in comparison to others that I panic. I can't breathe. I scream and sob.

So where do I find my source for self-love?

In quiet moments of clarity I remember a certain verse from the Dao de Jing that has stuck with me since I first read the text as a 14-year-old girl:

> *When you are content to be simply yourself*
> *and don't compare or compete,*
> *everybody will respect you.*

Peace really begins within ourselves, and we will never find it by seeking that which others have. So I take a deep breath. And in these moments, I remember that these perceptions I have of others are...illusions. I see others through my own skewed vision based on my own insecurities.

I have discovered ways to cultivate self-love through positive thinking and developing habits that express my own self worth. These principles have helped me actively practice the act of self-love. I'd like to share them with you.

Staying grounded: When my mind races with insecurity, I take a moment to remember what's really important in life and to count my blessings. In reality, we all struggle and as real as your problems may seem, you also have many countless blessings. Focusing on those blessings in your life will keep your life in perspective and attract more positive energy.

Keep it simple: What does your day look like? Wake up, go to work, make lunch, go home, workout, go grocery shopping, cook, clean, and on and on? We build our lives so as to fill up time with no space for ourselves. Ladies, before we drive ourselves crazy, take a deep breath, relax, and discover what it means to just be. Breathe into the simplicity of a quiet existence. Minimize your possessions, slow down, make more time for yourself, and focus on the contentment of living simply in the present moment.

Accept conflict with an open and honest heart: In life we inevitably encounter toxic situations: an abusive boss, a critical friend, a competitive co-worker, a relationship with someone who doesn't love you as much as you deserve. These situations come into our lives. We cannot control that. But what we can control is our perspective and how we deal with them.

When a conflict arises, speak your truth with diplomacy and share your perspective with grace. Honor yourself by learning to say no and set boundaries. If a situation does not improve, trust yourself to say "enough," and let go of that which no longer serves you. Foster mutually fulfilling relationships at all levels and let go of those that bring harm.

Acceptance and letting go: Everything changes, including ourselves. We try to stop it. We build a false sense of security according to the relationship we're in or the job we have. As we age, we struggle to maintain our ideal weight or youthful appearance.

Learn to love yourself by accepting who you are in this present moment. Spend less time criticizing and more time praising yourself for your many beautiful qualities. If you can be non-judgmental with yourself, then that's the key to loving others.

When I let go, I can feel the shift, where I rest in the moment and worry less about the distant future. I let go of the person I think I am and allow myself to grow into the person I'm meant to become.

These transitions help us live in the present. Take the time to learn to let go and be completely present. Enable yourself to live in the flow instead of frustration. We can figure it all out as we go along.

Do what you love: If I'm going to spend most of my time working, I need to enjoy it. Express yourself in creative freedom. Ask yourself, what makes you shine? If you can't do it now, begin to set aside a little time each week toward achieving your long-term goal.

Rather than compare yourself to others, honor yourself. Transcend the pressures, standards, and expectations we put on ourselves when comparing ourselves to others. Let go of inhibitive social expectations or perceived behavioral requirements set by others. Instead act in a way that is right for you, that is practicing self-love.

When we love ourselves, the rest falls into place. The more you love yourself, the more love you have to give to others.

The Bruises Will Heal.
The Scars Will Fade.

by Kelsey Consciousness

The bruises will heal. The scars will fade.

Over time, slowly but surely they will fade until they disappear.

There will be a day when they don't even cross my mind because the last time I saw them was over a month ago. Standing in the shower, looking down at my arms and reliving the moment when the nurse brought in a needle and told me it was Heprin.

I politely refuse.

She insists, it's to prevent blood clots. To prevent my 20-something-year-old body, that eats well, is active, regenerative, and capable of cleansing its own blood, from blood clots. I politely refuse again and she insists further, jabbing the needle into my flesh. And there's the bruise from the IV that put me under, kept me unconscious through another surgery.

I gently wash my tender, aching body as I see beyond the bruises demanding attention on my arms, although not before contemplating what others who don't know me may think when they see the large dark marks on my inner elbows, arms, and hands.

My fingers are light to touch the sensitive skin I am living in. Everything hurts: the water streaming down; my breath quivering in and out restrained by the weakness of my reawakening lungs after anesthesia; the swelling of my skin and the bloating of my insides.

Pressure.

Pressure to exist in this weakened state. I notice my newly stitched flesh isn't looking so healthy, greying around the incisions and decaying away rather than fusing in bright reds and pinks. I shudder to my bones as I'm overcome with a feeling of frailness, shrinking inside myself a little. Wanting to escape the thoughts and sensations of self-rejection consuming my being. I inhale deeply and straighten my spine pushing through the pain, expanding my chest and standing strong in the stream of the flowing water, banishing thoughts of inadequacy and illness from my space entirely.

I am healing; this is progress in the process.

"Every little cell in my body is happy, every little cell in my body is well." I sing myself this sweet little mantra— something I learned from a friend. The power lies in my thoughts about my situation, so I struggle to replace all negative thoughts with ones of self-love, acceptance, and health.

"You're beautiful and healing perfectly!" I exclaim to myself boldly, but then tears begin to fall. Is it because I don't believe this or because I know it to be true and my current state depicts otherwise? Despite the healing that will come through the passage of time I wish I could fast forward into the future where I am not weak.

But I'm free, not stuck in a lifeless sterile building hooked up to monitors and medications and being fed dead nutrients. I'm alive, I'm rebuilding myself, after another rendezvous with the devil dancing in the shadows of hell, I'm in Eden and I'm awakening to a new spring, slowly coming back to life and feeling all of the blessings from the earth, moon, and the stars. I feel like a leaf being blown in the breezes of shifting energy, from below, above, rolling in and out with the tides. Never resisting, just swaying in the breezes as they come.

At this very second I am tender, I am frail, I am breakable.

My body is but a glimpse of my inner workings. I feel that if my bruises, scars and stitches would represent how fragile my interior was, my whole body would be a walking display of destruction. I've been shaken to the core once again, present awareness brought back into the temporal.

The impermanence of life and my body.

Appreciation for all the joys of life, knowing that they too are temporary.

In acceptance I dance through the waves of highs and lows.

The process of regeneration and restoration on so many levels.

Maybe as I lay on my back, close my eyes, taking slow deep breaths, in the silence of my aloneness I'll escape. I can relax and feel at ease. I sit with my thoughts and memories, and I let them go. I am present to my aches, pains and stiffness, but I also let that go. I fantasize about the day, hopefully soon, when I'll be running and jumping and bending in every way imaginable without so much as a hint of discomfort.

But for now, I am meant to sit with all of these stirrings, crazy thoughts and emotions and pains. Harsh reminders of my undeniable humanity, because often I like to contemplate in realms beyond my biological disposition.

I get to sit with the insecurities. The ones about my body that I thought I had overcome.

I get to sit with the uprising of negative emotions, fierce anger and irritability. Or sullen sadness with underlying depression, or sometimes unswayable indifference. My logical mind debates if it's from the chemical alterations of medications purging from the body or possibly the extreme detachment I've adopted towards all things mutable; the only conclusion to draw from this reality –brought plainly visible by my own mortality – is that it's probably both.

I get to hang out with the feeling of being inadequate, unable, and limited.

When I long to feel invincible. I get to contemplate if these feelings are just old programmed ways of knowing myself coming back to haunt me with the familiar pain of 13 surgeries past. Or if they are entirely new beasts finding refuge in my compromised body, mind, and spirit. Either way, I sit with the feelings of not knowing who I am in moments of anger, fear, or pain. The way I behave and the way I feel in my heart don't match. The things I say cause me more pain in the moments after than I had felt before. Shadow aspects lashing out in the midst of their awakening, full of life energy, draining me of my connection to truth, beauty, and love.

Stuck in an illusion of suffering.

I sit with the self-sabotage.

I sit with the unfulfilling feeling left after I realize no amount of self-destruction can validate something that isn't true. It can make me believe for a moment that yes, it's true, I am inadequate; see, look, it's proof. Proof in the scars, the stitches, and proof in the mind that swirls with chaos. But I know the truth deep down.

I know that the way I am being is not who I truly am. I wallow in the self-created misery because I excuse myself to

116

do so; I permit myself to be a victim, circumstantially of course. Plus, I justify in retrospect, how would I know who I truly am and what I am not, if not through experience and recognition of what's truth and what's illusion. Relation in the contrast.

It's all part of the process. The process of living. Life is beautiful, lovely, exciting, entrancing, romantic, and joyful.

But life is also painful, disconnecting, lonely, mournful suffrage.

Experiencing these times when the grass sure seems greener somewhere else, but finding the gratitude and connection in fleeting moments of sanity, of peace amongst the chaos.

Life often seems unreal in the magnificence of beauty. We live in a fantasy or faraway land, finding ourselves reveling; how can this be real life? It's too beautiful, too magical! And then it seems all too real in the moments of disdain, times that feel like endless suffering with no completion in sight, in drastic contrast to the moments spent floating on air.

It's all life, all equal, all necessary. The craziness, insanity, self-destruction and observation and reflection upon it. It's like moss on a rolling stone, slowing you down as you accumulate wisdom with experience, enriching your deep rooted presence in this life, in all if its glory.

I've learned to take the good with the bad, love the bad with the good.

Love myself in all forms, always transforming.

Even when I feel stuck in a moment, nothing is ever stagnant, and it's only within an attachment to what once was or what will possibly be in the future, that suffering becomes the primary state of being. It's all flowing, always changing, and I am grateful for that. I am grateful for today, however it turns out. I am grateful for my pain and grateful for the day that will eventually arrive when my bruises are gone and the scars fade, and only beauty and love remains.

MEET THE AUTHORS

Susan Araujo

Suzie is an Earth Angel sent to show compassion to everyone including people, animals, and plants. She has a love for music, children, and nature and can be often found chanting, singing, or doing yoga. She completed her yoga teacher training at I Love Yoga Studio in Dania, FL, and recently finished her YogaMusic Kids certification so she can teach yoga and music to the little beings of this world. Suzie is a sensitive lightworker who is in touch with the flow and energy of the universe. She used to think of it as a bad thing but now she embraces her sensitive spirit. She loves to dance, sing, love, and buzzzzzzzzzz.

Leilla Blackwell

Leilla Blackwell is a Certified Strategic Intervention Life Coach specializing in Love & Intimacy. In addition to direct coaching, she provides group coaching for women through her BLISSful Woman membership group, and for men through her PASSIONate Man program. She is a contributing writer for YourTango an online magazine, and hosts The Pleasure Map show on the Own Your Power Radio Network. She celebrates over 25 years with her husband, as together they live an inspired life with their three children. You can find out more about Leilla on her website www.LeillaBlackwell.com.

Kelsey Cavanagh

many different culture

Kelsey is native to the northern woods and coast of Maine. Many challenges with her health from a young age led her on a path seeking healing. Through her studies and practice of yoga, meditation, Reiki, and plant medicine she was able to heal herself from a serious illness, and continues in furthering her studies to help others on their path of healing. She now travels the world, continuing her learning and sharing of healing from

© Yanni De Melo

Marny Darius

I was born in Suriname, a country in the Northern part of South America and have lived in Florida for 19 years now. Throughout this life journey I've been through many fortunate and unfortunate circumstances, which have pointed me in a direction towards self-realization, growth and wisdom. All challenges have been teachings that have led and encouraged me to develop spiritual awareness. Because of this, I've been blessed to reach a level of spiritual awareness and realize my Divine purpose in life, which is to be at service to those who strive for a new way of life by assisting them to recognize their Divine existence. I empower and offer spiritual guidance, Energy Healing, Meditation and Food Therapy. I light the world by having compassion for all beings included animals and the planet, and love unconditionally. Namaste!

Zayna de Gaia

Zayna de Gaia is a life coach, author, speaker and teacher of teachers. She's passionate about yoga, meditation, empowering people to live their best life and the ongoing orgasms of being ALIVE! Zayna is the founder of Teen Whisperer International, committed to bridging the language barrier between teens and their parents via a holistic approach emphasizing communication and love. She is also the host of her own podcast radio and YouTube show: ZNation where she welcomes many inspiring guests who will leave you thinking "The world IS changing! There ARE people doing great things in the world!" She's is a yoga teacher and trainer, Reiki healer and practitioner and world renowned author of the book, *Thank you for HPV: A simple guide to healing yourself.* Find out more about the scrumptious details of these exciting projects at www.znationradio.com.

Allison Dienstman

American born, but a citizen of the world, with a commitment to life experience, Allison is a lover of language, travel, music, fashion, and cooking. Above all, she is an optimist. She has practiced yoga and studied eastern philosophy for over 12 years. Currently, she works as a writer for various projects. For more of her writing, visit her professional website or her blog **Olive Vintage**.

Milina Franke

© Jaamal Clark

I Am Milina.
I Am "Delightful."
You can find me whilst engulfed in "procrastination."
Outta such Wanderings,
We stumble upon meandering
Musings of Musical Miracles.
Between Breaths,
I Find Myself
Shining Brightly with your Presence.

It is with Written Word
I Explore,
Staying Sane
Long Enough to Revert
Back into Child-Like Stages.
Words Reflect Ageless
Truth of Sages.

All Beloved Friends and Family Along the Path:
Bula

Stephanie Loewenstern

Stephanie is a youthful, free spirit, self-love junkie who works in the staffing industry and teaches yoga. She received her 200YTT from Anuttara Yoga Shala in Deerfield Beach, FL. Stephanie has many passions including writing from her heart and her articles have appeared on **Found-My-Light.com**. She stands for a world that is abundant, adventurous, loving, peaceful, and free. When not teaching yoga, Stephanie spends her free time with her friends and family and loves to play on the beach, explore new activities and travel.

Emily Sunset Martinez

Emily Sunset Martinez is a yoga teacher, and radio producer. She is passionate about all things in life and empowering others to build a strong relationship of self love by holding space for others to explore those under layers of themselves. "I have always had a desire to throw myself into different societies, live and learn what they do. By doing that you not only learn about yourself, but you humble yourself to see how colorful this world really is." Growing up she faced many odds; from being born deaf, to obesity, and mental health issues. This has pushed her to follow her bliss and learn to let go of fear. She knew that she needed to find her voice so she can give voice to the invisible. So she decided to take a sabbatical from university to do much need exploration of herself which lead her to I Love Yoga Studio. She admits when she started training her intentions were not to become a yoga teacher; it was more like rehab for the soul. Now she teaches Hatha Yoga at I Love Yoga Studio and blogs on her Facebook page *Sunset Open your Heart*. You can also catch her working her producer skills for ZNation, a radio show about consciousness and making a difference on So Flo radio.

Jemine Omabegho

©Victoria Harding

As a 30 something life servant to feline royalty, She-Ra and Maximus, Jemine Omabegho has been finding the time to explore cooking gluten-free and lactose-free as well as having a great adventure in Chicago. When the princess and prince allow Jemine out of the house each morning, she becomes a project manager managing financial technology projects in EMV migration. Her goals are simple: continued contentment and happiness and the ability to be at peace as a single woman .

Karina Rosado

Karina is a Holistic Healer and Spiritual Reader amongst other things. She discovered her love of yoga in September 2005, and has since taught energy yoga, Qui Gong, and healing Martial Arts. She continues to practice on and off and recently completed a yoga teacher training at I love Yoga in Dania Beach, FL. Karina discovered her innate ability to heal others through Spiritual Energy work, and can tap in to other people's energy bodies and emotions, and release or shift unwanted energy stuck in one's body. She also communicates with Angels and spirit guides to give guidance to others. She studied Business Administration with a concentration in International Business, and graduated from Salem State College in May 2006. In 2013 she attended the Aveda Institute where she studied Esthetics and Massage Therapy. She hopes to travel the world and open up a boutique where she can incorporate fun and funky items along with offering her healing services for those in need. You can also reach her at www.healingformeandyou.com.

Ta-Shana Taylor

Ta-Shana is a geoscience educator who lives in Miami, Fl. Teaching people about the environment so they can connect with, and protect, our planet is her life's work. When she's not doing that, she's writing about her experiences as a woman of color or writing about sword-wielding women who kick butt and save the day.

Claudia Zebersky

Claudia Zebersky is a brand strategist, designer and creator of Purplewing Studio. A brand strategy and boutique design studio that guides and inspires entrepreneurs to discover their essence and build inspiring and meaningful personal and corporate brands that are in alignment with their soul's purpose.

Claudia Zebersky Is a charismatic, driven and creative woman, passionate about the art of living, spirituality and raising the consciousness of women. Claudia co-hosts monthly conscious women circles called "Red Tents" that create safe and nurturing environments where women can learn, grow and transform into the most beautiful expression of themselves. She's an avid student of heart-centered studies, Goddess Apprentice, lover of life, mother of two, committed to fulfilling her purpose, making a positive impact in the world and living the life of her wildest dreams.

Connect with her directly at claudia@purplewingstudio.com and find her work at **purplewingstudio.com**.

ABOUT THE EDITOR

Suki Eleuterio is a creative goddess, lightworker, and yogini who is dedicated to sharing love and happiness with the world. Suki knows her life mission is to help others remember that which they already know: that we are nothing but Divine Love. In 2010 she began her blog, **Sookton.com**, which has gone on to win several blogger awards. She has also created **Found-My-Light.com**, a community of lightworkers and conscious creators. Suki leads chakra, Shamanic, and yoga workshops in South Florida and online and has appeared on television and radio shows. Along with her business partner, Karen Bryce, she created "Soul Conversations," a sacred program that encourages women to speak their truths and uncover the layers of their soul. She is currently working on a book on spirituality called *No Fear in Spirit: How to Let Go of Anxiety and Follow Your Soul Path.* When she is not writing, leading a workshop, or on the yoga mat she is spending time with her loving family: Rob (her husband), Mishka (her daughter), and Lola (her fur baby).

ABOUT THE PHOTOGRAPHER

Susy Foltz is a photographer, interior decorator, Feng Shui practitioner, Reiki Master, and minimalist.

Having lived in 17 countries, her eclectic style has been inspired and influenced by the colorful, multi-cultural diversity she has embraced along the way.

As a mother of five, she understands the importance of organizing your space in a practical way that allows for fast-paced living. Her mission is to help her clients experience the freedom that is possible when they simplify and create home sanctuaries.

As a healer, she supports her clients compassionately in the art of letting go so they can heal themselves as the energy in their homes is transformed.

She loves showing women how to embrace their inner beauty through the art of photography.

You can see more of her photography at **www.susyfoltzphotography.com**.

WHAT'S YOUR STORY?

Do you want to be part of *She Loved Herself Volume II*? Do you have a story to tell about how you learned to love yourself?

Visit **www.sookton.com/contact** and fill out your contact information and the idea for your story. You may be considered as an author for a future collection of essays.

"The divine light in me recognizes
and bows to the divine light in you."

Namaste

70560842R00078

Made in the USA
Columbia, SC
09 May 2017